Patrick Fitzgerald, Marie McCullagh and Carol Tabor

English for
ICT
STUDIES

in Higher Education Studies
Course Book

Series editor: Terry Phillips

English for Specific Academic Purposes

Garnet
EDUCATION

Published by
Garnet Publishing Ltd.
8 Southern Court
South Street
Reading RG1 4QS, UK

First published 2011

ISBN 978 1 85964 519 2

British Cataloguing-in-Publication Data
A catalogue record for this book is available from the British Library.

Production
Series editor: Terry Phillips
Project management: Vale Dominguez, Claire Forsyth
Editorial team: Kirsten Campbell, Claire Forsyth, Amanda Ilic, Karen Kinnair-Pugh
Specialist review: John Hawker
Design: Henry Design Associates and Mike Hinks
Photography: Sally Henry and Trevor Cook, alamy.com, clipart.com, corbis,com, dreamstime.com, gettyimages.com, istockphoto.com

Audio recorded at Motivation Sound Studios produced by EFS Television Production Ltd.

The authors and publisher would like to thank the following for permission to reproduce copyright material:
Image no. 7 on page 7 reproduced with kind permission of Symantec Corporation; Image C on page 10 from www.euroncap.com; Image 2 on page 15 from www.apple.com; Image no. 4 on page 23 reproduced with kind permission of Nokia; Screenshot on page 24 from SysTools; Results listings on page 35 with kind permission of Google; Image no. 1 on page 39 reproduced with kind permission of Steven Sengel, www.oldcomputers.net; Image no. 3 on page 39 reproduced with kind permission of The Internet Encyclopaedia of Science; Graphs on page 39 reproduced with kind permission of Ray Kurzweil; Image no. 1 on page 40 reproduced with kind permission of The International Slide Rule Museum; Image no. 3 on page 40 reproduced with kind permission of the National Archives, Image no. 4 on page 40 from www.ibm.com; Image no. 2 on page 43 reproduced with kind permission of Bill Degnan, www.vintage-computer.net; Image no. 3 on page 43 from www.cisco.com; Image no. 4 on page 43 reproduced with kind permission of Intel Corporation; Image no. 5 on page 43 reproduced with kind permission of Belkin Limited; Image no. 6 on page 43 reproduced with kind permission of George Michael, www.computer-history.info; Image no. 7 on page 43 from CORE Memory/Mark Richards; Image no. 8 on page 43 from www.ibm.com; Images on page 49 from YouTube, Flickr®, Blogger and Wikpedia; page 58 (c) 2010 Netscape Communications Corporation. Used with permission.; page 59 My SQL is a registered trademark of Oracle and/or its affiliates. Used with permission.; Images on page 59 from The Apache Software Foundation, www.apache.org, Linux, www.linux.co.uk and The PHP Group, www.php.net; Screenshots C on page 63 reproduced with kind permission of Microsoft and Ubuntu; Images no. 1 and 2 on page 74 reproduced with kind permission of Nokia; Image no. 3 on page 74 reproduced with kind permission of Hewlett-Packard Development Company, L.P.; Image no. 4 on page 74 from Toshiba Europe GmbH; Form on page 79 contains public sector information licensed under the Open Government Licence v1.0; Text on page 83 © Cengage Learning; Image C on page 87 from www.bodetech.com; Images on page 91 reproduced with kind permission of Graham Turner/Guardian News & Media Ltd 2006.

Every effort has been made to trace copyright holders and we apologize in advance for any unintentional omission. We will be happy to insert the appropriate acknowledgements in any subsequent editions.

Printed and bound in Lebanon by International Press: interpress@int-press.com

Introduction

English for ICT Studies is designed for students who plan to take an ICT course entirely or partly in English. The principal aim of *English for ICT Studies* is to teach students to cope with input texts, i.e., listening and reading, in the discipline. However, students will be expected to produce output texts in speech and writing throughout the course.

The syllabus focuses on key vocabulary for the discipline and on words and phrases commonly used in academic English. It covers key facts and concepts from the discipline, thereby giving students a flying start for when they meet the same points again in their faculty work. It also focuses on the skills that will enable students to get the most out of lectures and written texts. Finally, it presents the skills required to take part in seminars and tutorials and to produce essay assignments.

English for ICT Studies comprises:

- student Course Book including audio transcripts and wordlist
- the Teacher's Book, which provides detailed guidance on each lesson, full answer keys, audio transcripts and extra photocopiable resources
- audio CDs with lecture and seminar excerpts

English for ICT Studies has 12 units, each of which is based on a different aspect of ICT. Odd-numbered units are based on listening (lecture/seminar extracts). Even-numbered units are based on reading.

Each unit is divided into four lessons:

Lesson 1: vocabulary for the discipline; vocabulary skills such as word-building, use of affixes, use of synonyms for paraphrasing

Lesson 2: reading or listening text and skills development

Lesson 3: reading or listening skills extension. In addition, in later units, students are introduced to a writing assignment which is further developed in Lesson 4; in later listening units, students are introduced to a spoken language point (e.g., making an oral presentation at a seminar) which is further developed in Lesson 4

Lesson 4: a parallel listening or reading text to that presented in Lesson 2 which students have to use their new skills (Lesson 3) to decode; in addition, written or spoken work is further practised

The last two pages of each unit, *Vocabulary bank* and *Skills bank*, are a useful summary of the unit content.

Each unit provides between 4 and 6 hours of classroom activity with the possibility of a further 2–4 hours on the suggested extra activities. The course will be suitable, therefore, as the core component of a faculty-specific pre-sessional or foundation course of between 50 and 80 hours.

It is assumed that prior to using this book students will already have completed a general EAP (English for Academic Purposes) course such as *Skills in English* (Garnet Publishing, up to the end at least of Level 3), and will have achieved an IELTS level of at least 5.

For a list of other titles in this series, see www.garneteducation.com/

Book map

Unit	Topics
1 What is ICT? Listening · Speaking	• defining ICT • introduction to different aspects of ICT
2 ICT in the workplace Reading · Writing	• impact of ICT on business, including communication, information management and product design • impact of ICT on the nature of work, including teleworking and outsourcing
3 Introduction to ICT systems Listening · Speaking	• embedded and general purpose systems • data storage and management • control systems • communication systems • functions of ICT systems (data capture, processing and output)
4 ICT in education Reading · Writing	• use of computers and the Internet in research and learning • computer-assisted learning (CAL), virtual learning environments (VLEs) and their impact on teaching
5 The history of ICT Listening · Speaking	• key stages in the development of the computer (inventions and innovations) • development of computer components (input, output, processing and storage) • foundations of the Internet
6 The Internet Reading · Writing	• Internet protocols and data transfer • Web 2.0 and the future of the Internet • social networking services (SNS)
7 Software development Listening · Speaking	• development methods and processes • waterfall, iterative and prototyping models • planning the development process • open source software
8 Efficiency in computer systems Reading · Writing	• efficiency in computer systems • reliability, security, speed and cost
9 Human-computer interaction (HCI) Listening · Speaking	• importance and scope of HCI • aspects of human sciences and computer sciences • different types of interface • hardware and software
10 E-commerce and e-government Reading · Writing	• types of e-commerce: B2B, B2C, C2C, B2G • barriers to adoption of e-commerce
11 Computing and ethics Listening · Speaking	• laws and regulations, including copyright • principles and ethics, including privacy and surveillance • the role of hacking
12 ICT in the future Reading · Writing	• virtual and mirror worlds • augmented reality (AR) • lifelogging • using technological growth curves to predict future development

Vocabulary focus	Skills focus		Unit
• words from general English with a special meaning in ICT • prefixes and suffixes	Listening	• preparing for a lecture • predicting lecture content from the introduction • understanding lecture organization • choosing an appropriate form of notes • making lecture notes	**1**
	Speaking	• speaking from notes	
• English–English dictionaries: headwords · definitions · parts of speech · phonemes · stress markers · countable/uncountable · transitive/intransitive	Reading	• using research questions to focus on relevant information in a text • using topic sentences to get an overview of the text	**2**
	Writing	• writing topic sentences • summarizing a text	
• stress patterns in multi-syllable words • prefixes	Listening	• preparing for a lecture • predicting lecture content • making lecture notes • using different information sources	**3**
	Speaking	• reporting research findings • formulating questions	
• computer jargon • abbreviations and acronyms • discourse and stance markers • verb and noun suffixes	Reading	• identifying topic development within a paragraph • using the Internet effectively • evaluating Internet search results	**4**
	Writing	• reporting research findings	
• word sets: synonyms, antonyms, etc. • the language of trends • common lecture language	Listening	• understanding 'signpost language' in lectures • using symbols and abbreviations in note-taking	**5**
	Speaking	• making effective contributions to a seminar	
• synonyms, replacement subjects, etc., for sentence-level paraphrasing	Reading	• locating key information in complex sentences	**6**
	Writing	• reporting findings from other sources: paraphrasing • writing complex sentences	
• compound nouns • fixed phrases from ICT • fixed phrases from academic English • common lecture language	Listening	• understanding speaker emphasis	**7**
	Speaking	• asking for clarification • responding to queries and requests for clarification	
• synonyms • nouns from verbs • definitions • common 'direction' verbs in essay titles (*discuss, analyze, evaluate*, etc.)	Reading	• understanding dependent clauses with passives	**8**
	Writing	• paraphrasing • expanding notes into complex sentences • recognizing different essay types/structures: descriptive · analytical · comparison/evaluation · argument • writing essay plans • writing essays	
• fixed phrases from ICT • fixed phrases from academic English	Listening	• using the Cornell note-taking system • recognizing digressions in lectures	**9**
	Speaking	• making effective contributions to a seminar • referring to other people's ideas in a seminar	
• 'neutral' and 'marked' words • fixed phrases from ICT • fixed phrases from academic English	Reading	• recognizing the writer's stance and level of confidence or tentativeness • inferring implicit ideas	**10**
	Writing	• writing situation–problem–solution–evaluation essays • using direct quotations • compiling a bibliography/reference list	
• words/phrases used to link ideas (*moreover, as a result,* etc.) • stress patterns in noun phrases and compounds • fixed phrases from academic English • words/phrases related to ethics in computing	Listening	• recognizing the speaker's stance • writing up notes in full	**11**
	Speaking	• building an argument in a seminar • agreeing/disagreeing	
• verbs used to introduce ideas from other sources (*X contends/suggests/asserts that* …) • linking words/phrases conveying contrast (*whereas*), result (*consequently*), reasons (*due to*), etc. • words for quantities (*a significant minority*)	Reading	• understanding how ideas in a text are linked	**12**
	Writing	• deciding whether to use direct quotation or paraphrase • incorporating quotations • writing research reports • writing effective introductions/conclusions	

1 WHAT IS ICT?

A Read the text. The red words are probably familiar to you in general English. But can you think of a different meaning for each word used in an ICT context? Change the form if necessary (e.g., change a noun into a verb).

> Anna phoned the language school to say she had a virus and was too ill to work. She found a little bit of chocolate in the fridge, plugged in her CD player, and sat down to browse through her TV magazine and play with her pet mouse. On the table there was a menu for a local Chinese restaurant. Anna was choosing lunch when the postman arrived with a package addressed to her. She stepped out to get it and the door closed behind her. Anna realized her keys were inside the house and she was locked out.

B Read these sentences from ICT texts. Complete each sentence with one of the red words from Exercise A. Change the form if necessary.

1 Select an option from the drop-down _____ .

2 The smallest unit of data in a computer is a _____ , short for *binary digit.*

3 Anti _____ software protects computers from infection.

4 High-level programming _____ , such as C and C++, are made up of letters, numbers and symbols.

5 To view information on the Internet you need a web _____ .

6 Click on the _____ twice to open the program.

7 This software _____ includes a number of programs that businesses will find useful.

8 One way to protect data is to encrypt it so that only someone with the correct _____ , or password, can open it.

9 Most Internet _____ begin www.

10 You may need to install a _____ to play music or watch films on your computer.

C Study the words in box a.

1 What is the connection between all the words?

2 What is the base word in each case?

3 What do we call the extra letters?

4 What is the meaning of each prefix?

5 Can you think of another word with each prefix?

> **a** antivirus centimetre gigabyte
> hyperlink Internet kilobit
> microchip millisecond
> miscalculate output restart
> subnetwork superhighway
> telecommunications undetected

D Study the words in box b.

1 What is the connection between all the words?

2 What is the base word in each case?

3 What do we call the extra letters?

4 What effect do the extra letters have on the base word?

5 Can you think of another word with each suffix?

> **b** classify computerize connector
> developer digital downloading
> electronic instruction management
> mobility paperless performance
> software technology variable

E Use words from this page to label the pictures on the opposite page. Add labels for other items in the pictures.

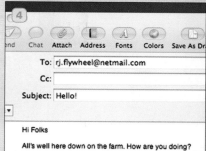

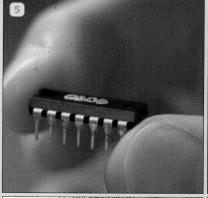

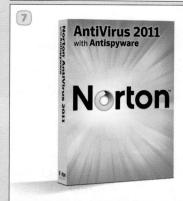

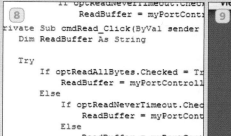

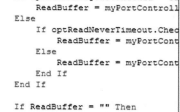

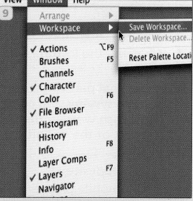

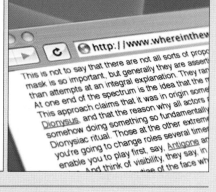

A You are a student in the ICT Faculty of Hadford University. The title of your first lecture is *What is ICT?*

  1 Write a definition of ICT.

  2 How can you prepare for this lecture? Make some notes.

B 🎧 Listen to Part 1 of the talk. What does the lecturer say about ICT? Tick the best choice.

  a It is about computers. ____

  b It is about information. ____

  c It is about playing computer games. ____

  d It is more than just using a computer. ✓

C In Part 2 of the talk, the lecturer mentions *virus* and *driver*.

  1 What do these words mean in the context of ICT?

  2 🎧 Listen and check your ideas.

D In Part 3 of the talk, the lecturer describes different places where ICT has an impact.

  1 How many different places can you think of?

  2 What are some of the technologies used in each place?

  3 🎧 Listen and check your ideas.

  4 What will the lecturer talk about next?

E 🎧 In the final part of the talk, the lecturer talks about information systems and communication systems. Listen and mark each word in the box **E** if it is an example and **D** if it is part of the definition.

> communicate ____   data ____   e-mail ____
> mobile phones ____   process ____
> store ____   using technology ____   web page ____

F Draw a flowchart to illustrate ICT. Use some of the words from Exercise E in your flowchart.

G Describe ICT, using your flowchart.

H Look back at your notes from Exercise A. Did you predict:

  • the main ideas?

  • most of the special vocabulary?

See *Skills bank*

1.3 Extending skills

lecture organization • choosing the best form of notes

A What can you …

1 develop?
2 process?
3 connect?

4 assemble?
5 install?
6 launch?

7 program?
8 computerize?
9 monitor?

B How can you organize information in a lecture? Match the beginnings and endings.

1 question and i
2 problem and h
3 classification and b
4 advantages and c
5 comparison and a
6 cause and d
7 sequence of e
8 stages of a g
9 theories or opinions then f

a contrast
b definition
c disadvantages
d effect
e events
f supporting information
g process
h solution
i answer

C How can you record information during a lecture? Match the illustrations with the words and phrases in the box.

tree diagram   flowchart   headings and notes   spidergram   table   timeline   two columns
   2   1   5   7   4   6   3

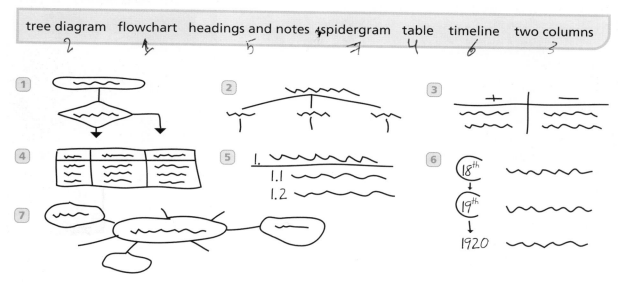

D Match each organization of information in Exercise B with a method of note-taking from Exercise C. You can use one method for different types of organization.

E 🎧 Listen to five lecture introductions. Choose a possible way to take notes from Exercise C in each case.

Example:

You hear: *In today's session, we're going to look at ICT in business. We will be looking at a car manufacturing company and discussing four areas of business: administration, finance, research and development, and operations, to see what happens in each area and how ICT supports workers in these areas.*

You choose: *tree diagram*

A Study the pictures.

1 What do pictures 1–5 show? Use words from the box.

2 What does each picture A–C show?

engine rocket bug e-mail waterfall

B 🎧 Cover the opposite page. Listen to the lecture introductions from Lesson 1.3 again. Make an outline on a separate sheet of paper for each introduction.

C Look at your outline for each lecture. What do you expect the lecturer to talk about in the lecture? In what order?

D 🎧 Listen to the next part of each lecture. Complete your notes.

E Uncover the opposite page. Check your notes with the model notes. Are yours the same or different?

F Work in pairs.

1 Use the notes on the opposite page. Reconstruct one lecture.

2 Give the lecture to another pair.

1

ICT in business

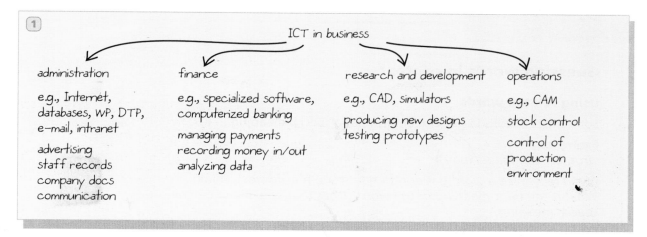

administration

e.g., Internet, databases, WP, DTP, e-mail, intranet

advertising
staff records
company docs
communication

finance

e.g., specialized software, computerized banking

managing payments
recording money in/out
analyzing data

research and development

e.g., CAD, simulators

producing new designs
testing prototypes

operations

e.g., CAM

stock control

control of production environment

2

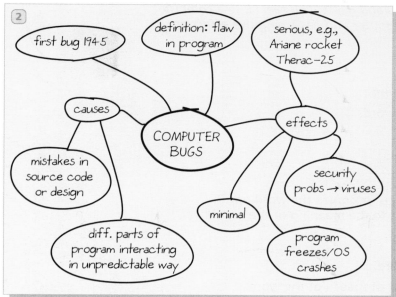

first bug 1945

definition: flaw in program

serious, e.g., Ariane rocket Therac-25

causes

COMPUTER BUGS

effects

mistakes in source code or design

security probs → viruses

minimal

diff. parts of program interacting in unpredictable way

program freezes/OS crashes

3

Info systems life cycle
Waterfall model

(Winston Royce 1970)

1 – requirements specification (systems analyst)

2 – systems + software design (software designer/architect)

3 – development + unit testing (programmers)

4 – integration + systems testing

5 – installation, operation and maintenance

4

Internet – how it began

1957 – Sputnik 1, US/Soviet Space Race begins
Advanced Research Projects Agency (ARPA) set up by US Gov.

1969 – ARPANET = small network of computers for use during nuclear attack

1972 – US scientists and academics using ARPANET

1973 – ARPANET used internationally
early 80s – Internet – worldwide network of computers for military use + academic/scientific research

1986 – general public begin using Internet
early 90s – Tim Berners-Lee invents HTML (diplays text+ images) + HTTP (information transfer)

2009 – over 1.7bn users (approx. 25% world's pop.)

5

CMC (computer-mediated communication)
Electronic mail (e-mail)
messages sent/received in digital form via

intranet
internal

limited access

external Internet
open

worldwide access

Advantages of e-mail
• easy
• fast
• messages cheap to send
• can attach files, e.g., docs, photos, video
• can send 1 message to many people

Disadvantages
• sometimes e-mails get lost
• set-up costs high (computer, etc.)
• information overload
• spam/junk mail
• viruses

Guessing words in context

Using related words

Sometimes a word in general English has a special meaning in ICT.

Examples:
virus, bit, language, mouse

If you recognize a word but don't understand it in context, think:
What is the basic meaning of the word? Does that help me understand the special meaning?

Example:
*A **virus** is something that **infects** you and makes you feel ill, so a **computer virus** is something that **infects** a computer and has a negative effect on how it works.*

Removing prefixes

A **prefix** = letters at the **start of a word**.

A prefix changes the meaning of a word.

Examples:
restart – start again
miscalculate – calculate wrongly

If you don't recognize a word, think:
Is there is a prefix? Remove it. Do you recognize the word now?
What does that prefix mean? Add it to the meaning of the word.

Removing suffixes

A **suffix** = letters at the **end of a word**.

A suffix sometimes changes the part of speech of the word.

Examples:
develop ➔ *developer* = verb ➔ noun
vary ➔ *variable* = verb ➔ adjective

A suffix sometimes changes the meaning **in a predictable way**.

Examples:
paper + less – without (paper)
vary + able – able to (vary)

If you don't recognize a word, think:
Is there a suffix? Remove it. Do you recognize the word now?
What does that suffix mean? Add it to the meaning of the word.

Making the most of lectures

Before a lecture ...

Plan
- Find out the topic of the lecture.
- Research the topic.
- Check the pronunciation of names and key words in English.

Prepare
- Get to the lecture room early.
- Sit where you can see and hear well.
- Bring any equipment you may need.
- Write the date, topic and name of the lecturer at the top of a sheet of paper.

During a lecture ...

Predict
- Listen carefully to the introduction. Think: *What kind of lecture is this?*
- Write an outline. Leave space for notes.
- Think of possible answers/solutions/effects, etc., while the lecturer is speaking.

Produce
- Write notes/copy from the board.
- Record sources – books/websites/names.
- At the end, ask the lecturer/other students for missing information.

Making perfect lecture notes

Choose the best way to record information from a lecture.

advantages and disadvantages	➔ two-column table
cause and effect	➔ spidergram
classification and definition	➔ tree diagram/spidergram
comparison and contrast	➔ table
facts and figures	➔ table
sequence of events	➔ timeline
stages of a process	➔ flowchart
question and answer	➔ headings and notes

Speaking from notes

Sometimes you have to give a short talk in a seminar on research you have done.
- Prepare the listeners with an introduction.
- Match the introduction to the type of information/notes.

2 ICT IN THE WORKPLACE

A How can an English–English dictionary help you understand and produce spoken and written English?

B Study the dictionary extract on the opposite page.

1 Why are the two words (top left and top right) important?
2 How many meanings does *information* have?
3 Why does the word *input* appear twice in **bold**?
4 What do we call someone who provides information?
5 What do the letters ICT stand for?
6 Where is the main stress on *inform*? What about *information*?
7 What part of speech is *internal*?
8 What is the pronunciation of *o* in each bold word in this extract?
9 Which is correct? *Bad information **is/are** responsible for many business failures.*
10 Can we write: *The manager spoke to his staff and informed.* Why (not)?

C Look at the bold words in the dictionary extract on the opposite page.

1 What order are they in?
2 Write the words in box a in the same order.

> **a** program   log   communication
> system   text   scan
> support   notebook   device   robot
> process   package   service

D Look at the top of this double page from an English–English dictionary.

1 Which word from box a will appear on these pages?
2 Think of words before and after some of the other words in box a.

software   symbol

E Look up the red words in box a.

1 How many meanings can you find for each word?
2 Which words are both a noun and a verb? What kind of verbs are they?
3 What kind of noun is each one?
4 How are the words used in ICT?

F Look up the green words in box a.

1 Where is the stress in each word?
2 What is the sound of the underlined letter(s) in each word?
3 How are the words used in ICT?

G Test each other on the words from box a. Give the dictionary definition of one of the words. Can your partner guess which word you are defining?

H Discuss the pictures on the opposite page using words from this lesson.

ICT
intranet

ICT /aɪ siː 'tiː/ *n* [U] *abb. for* **information and communications technology**

inform /ɪnˈfɔːm/ *v* [T] give someone facts: *He informed the staff of his decision.*

informant /ɪnˈfɔːmənt/ *n* [C] someone who gives information to others: *We collected information for our survey from 50 informants.*

information /ɪnfəˈmeɪʃn/ *n* [U] 1. facts about someone or something: *There is a lot of information about laptops in this magazine.* 2. data which is processed, stored, or transmitted by computer or electronic equipment: *The computer calculates the hours you work and uses this information to work out how much to pay you.*

information and communications technology /ɪnfəˈmeɪʃn ən kəmjuːnɪˈkeɪʃnz tekˈnɒlədʒi/ *n* [U] (the study of) computers and electronic equipment used to handle information or to communicate with others: *He teaches ICT at the university.*

information superhighway /ɪnfəˈmeɪʃn suːpəˈhaɪweɪ/ *n* [sing.] the network of information and communications systems, including satellite communications and the Internet, used to store and transfer information around the world.

input[1] /ˈɪnpʊt/ *n* [C or U] 1. data or information which is put into a computer: *There were several spelling mistakes in the input which caused some problems with our deliveries.* 2. the contribution that someone makes: *The manager thanked everyone for their input on the new project.* 3. the place where information enters a computer or electronic device: *The video and DVD inputs are at the back of the television.*

input[2] /ˈɪnpʊt/ *v* [T] put data into a computer so that it can be stored or processed: *I have to input customer details into the computer.*

input device /ˈɪnpʊt dɪˌvaɪs/ *n* [C] anything that allows data or information to be put into a computer, e.g., a keyboard.

internal /ɪnˈtɜːnl/ *adj* inside a person, thing, or organization: *We use the company intranet for internal communications.*

Internet /ˈɪntənet/ *n* [sing.] a public network which links computers around the world: *I did most of the research on the Internet.*

intranet /ˈɪntrənet/ *n* [C] a private network of computers, like the Internet, which can only be used by people in a particular company or organization.

A How do you use ICT in your work or studies? What are the advantages? Can you think of any disadvantages?

B Look at the pictures on this page.

  1 How is ICT being used in the pictures?

  2 Which picture shows people using ICT to communicate with other people?

  3 Which pictures show ICT systems doing work that people once did?

  4 How was this work done before ICT was introduced?

C You are going to read a text. What should you do before you read a text in detail? *See Skills bank*

D This text is about ICT in the workplace.

  1 Think of some research questions before you read.

  2 Compare your questions with those in the Hadford University assignment on this page.

E Study these topic sentences from the text and answer the questions below.

> ICT plays a key role in business today.

> Firstly, ICT is a faster and more efficient way for people to communicate.

> ICT is also used to input, store and manage information.

> Another area where ICT is important is the retail industry.

> Manufacturers use new technology to design and build products.

> New technology, then, offers a range of benefits.

> However, it is important to understand that there are costs as well as benefits.

> Modern technology is here to stay.

  1 What types of businesses are discussed?

  2 Where might you find the answer to each question in the Hadford University assignment? Where possible, write 1, 2 or 3 next to the topic sentence.

  3 What do you expect to find in the other paragraphs?

F Read the text on the opposite page and check your ideas.

See Skills bank

HADFORD *University*

Faculty: ICT

Assignment

Do some research into the use of ICT in the workplace.

Make notes to answer these questions.

1 How is ICT used in the workplace?

2 What are the advantages for businesses of using ICT?

3 What factors do businesses have to consider before they invest in ICT?

I(nformation and) C(ommunication) T(echnology) at Work

ICT plays a key role in business today. In fact, its use is now so widespread that it is difficult to succeed without it. Rapid developments in the ICT sector in the last two decades have produced a huge range of new products and services. These include products such as personal computers (PCs), notebooks and fax machines, and services such as e-mail, intranet and the Internet. Businesses of all sizes and types use computer-based systems like these because they offer a better way to work – one which can save time and money.

Firstly, ICT is a faster and more efficient way for people to communicate. Businesses no longer have to rely on slow postal services. They can send and receive information and documents by text, e-mail or fax. Video-conferencing means people do not need to travel long distances to attend meetings. ICT provides a way for people within an organization to contact each other quickly and share work. It also means that they can work with people around the world.

ICT is also used to input, store and manage information. One common use of office computers is to record, find and work with information. For example, businesses use word-processing (WP) or desktop publishing (DTP) packages to produce company documents, and databases to store customer details and produce mailing lists. In the past, these tasks took hours, days or even weeks and produced a lot of paperwork. With ICT they take less time and cost less. Such electronic systems also save storage space.

Another area where ICT is important is the retail industry. Most items on sale in shops have a small black and white label called a bar code. Many shops combine bar-coding with electronic point-of-sale (EPOS) systems. The customer takes an item to the cashier, who uses a scanning device to read the bar code and find out the price of the item. The EPOS system logs each sale and helps the shop manager to decide which products to reorder from the supplier. Some EPOS systems are even programmed to do the ordering.

Manufacturers use new technology to design and build products. At the design stage, they use computer-aided design (CAD) software to produce new ideas and designs. In the production stage, many companies use robots. These are machines that do the work of people, and are controlled by computer-assisted manufacturing (CAM) programs. Robots can carry out routine, complex and dangerous procedures. They can work 24 hours a day and the standard of their work remains constant because they do not get tired or bored. As a result, companies can improve their production rates without losing quality.

New technology, then, offers a range of benefits. Firstly, it saves time. Tasks that once took a long time to do by hand now take a fraction of that time. Secondly, ICT improves communication between people, speeding up business transactions and decision-making, and opening up new markets around the world. Thirdly, inexpensive ICT solutions can often replace expensive people. Consequently, companies can reduce the size of their workforce and their wage bills. Finally, ICT can increase the quantity and improve the quality of goods produced, which may also increase profits.

However, it is important to understand that there are costs as well as benefits. ICT systems can be very expensive. Companies have to choose systems which suit their needs and are cost-effective before investing in ICT. They have to consider several factors. Firstly, technology is constantly developing, which means that systems need to be regularly upgraded. Another issue is staff training. There is no point installing an ICT system if workers cannot use it. Lastly, there is the cost of technical support, such as a helpdesk, to ensure that everything runs well on a daily basis.

Modern technology is here to stay. It would be almost impossible to ignore computer-based systems or to return to working without them. However, successful use of ICT requires investment in both equipment and skills. Businesses of all sizes need to make the right choices because there are risks, as well as benefits, involved.

A Study the words in box a. They are all from the text in Lesson 2.2.

1 Look back at the text on page 17. Find the words which go together with the words in the box.

2 Do they make noun or verb phrases?

3 What is the meaning of each phrase? Look at the context and check with your dictionary if necessary.

> **a** key fax publishing store space combine logs routine reduce

B Study the words in box b. They are all from Lesson 2.2.

1 What is the base word in each case? What part of speech is the base word?

2 Does the prefix/suffix change the part of speech?

3 How does the prefix/suffix change the meaning of the base word?

> **b** Internet video-conferencing manager reorder communication upgrade impossible

C Look back at the text on page 17. After each topic sentence, how does the writer continue the paragraph? Choose one or more from the following list:

- defining and describing
- giving (an) example(s)
- restating the topic sentence
- giving a list of points
- giving more information
- concluding

D Write a summary of the text on page 17. Paraphrase the topic sentences. Add extra information and examples. **See Skills bank**

A Discuss these questions.

1 Can you remember how ICT is used in different types of businesses?

2 What are the benefits of using ICT?

3 What are the costs?

B The lecturer has asked you to do some research into *the changing nature of work*.

1 What effect has ICT had on the work that people do?

2 Think of good research questions before you read the text on the opposite page.

3 Look quickly at the text on the opposite page. What is the best way to record information while you are reading?

C Study the text on the opposite page.

1 Highlight the topic sentences.

2 Read each topic sentence. What will you find in the rest of the paragraph?

3 Which paragraph(s) will probably answer each research question? Read those paragraphs and make notes.

4 Have you got all the information you need? If not, read other paragraphs.

D Use the Internet to find out more about how work is changing because of ICT. Explain how this seems to fit an organization or a person that you know.

1 Make notes.

2 Write a series of topic sentences which summarize your findings.

3 Report back to the other students. Read out each topic sentence then add extra details.

Changing the way we work

In the past, many people stayed in the same job for their whole life. When ICT first appeared in the workplace, many people feared they would lose their jobs to machines. This was true in some cases. For example, robots have replaced large numbers of production line workers in the manufacturing industry. Service industries, such as banking, also cut jobs when they brought in automated systems. However, while technology has made some jobs disappear, at the same time it has created new types of employment. These include jobs in areas such as software engineering and website design. Nowadays, people have to prepare for change, possibly involving retraining more than once.

The introduction of modern technology has not caused high unemployment, but it has meant that workers need new skills. Many people have retrained so that they can find new work in customer service industries, like call centres. Some have moved into the ICT industry to work as developers or trainers. Others have learnt to do their old jobs in a new way. For example, typists and journalists now work with computers instead of typewriters. Some people find that new technology has changed their work and given them increased responsibilities. This can mean that their jobs are now much more interesting.

ICT is not only changing the nature of work, it is also starting to change *where* that work is done. Most office workers travel to and from work every day. Now companies are starting to look at the possibilities of teleworking, or telecommuting, where staff work at home or from a telecentre. They use computers and telecommunications equipment to stay in contact with their office.

Telework has advantages for both employers and employees. Firms save money because they do not need large offices. They can recruit people who live further away or who would find it difficult to work normal office hours: for example, women with children. However, it does mean that they lose direct control over their workers. Employees save time because they do not have to commute long distances and can organize their work to suit themselves. The disadvantage for teleworkers is that they work alone and may miss sharing ideas with their colleagues, or working as part of a team. They can also find it difficult to separate work and home life.

The same systems that allow people to work from home also allow employers to outsource work to cheaper areas. In Britain, firms have opened telecentres outside the major cities. They have opted for towns where office space and labour are not so expensive. However, there is no reason why work cannot be moved to cheaper parts of the world. Indeed, over the last few years, a number of multinational companies have closed call centres and data-processing centres in Britain and moved the work to India, where salaries are lower. More recently, however, some large UK companies have brought their operations back into the UK due to customer service issues. This is, perhaps, a good example of companies thinking about ICT in isolation without thinking of what's best for the business or their customers.

The increasing demand for good ICT skills in the workplace has also had an impact on the world of education. Many governments have responded by investing in new technology for schools so that pupils can learn both with and about computer-based systems. Universities now offer a whole range of ICT-related courses, which means that teachers have had to learn to use ICT to deliver lessons in the classroom or teach entire courses online. This kind of change is important because young people who have computer skills will have an advantage when it comes to finding work.

How, when and where we work is changing and will continue to change. Success depends ultimately on whether we accept or reject this change. People have to be more flexible about the hours they work and the type of work they do. Nowadays, job security no longer comes from finding a job and staying in that job for life. It comes from having the skills and flexibility to adapt to change and being prepared to learn new things.

Using your English–English dictionary

This kind of dictionary helps you actually **learn** English.

Using headwords and parts of speech

1 Find the correct **headword**.
These **bold** words in a dictionary are in alphabetical order. Look at the words on the top left and top right of the double page. Find a word which comes just before and after your word.

2 Find the correct **meaning**.
If there are different meanings of the word, they appear in a numbered list. Look at all the meanings before you choose the correct one in context.

3 Find the correct **part of speech**.
Sometimes the same headword appears more than once, followed by a small number. This means the word has more than one part of speech, e.g., *n* and *v*. Work out the part of speech before you look up a word.
Clues:
 • Nouns often come after articles (*a*/*an*/*the*) or adjectives.
 • Verbs come after nouns or pronouns.

Learning to pronounce words

The symbols after the headword show you how to pronounce the word. Learn these symbols (the key is usually at the front or the back of the dictionary).

The little line in the symbols shows you how to stress the word.

Example:
/ɪnˈfɔːm/ but /ɪnfəˈmeɪʃn̩/

Learning to use words correctly in context

Nouns can be **countable** or **uncountable**. This information is important for using articles and verb forms (e.g., *is*/*are*) correctly. Look for the symbol [**C**] or [**U**].

Some verbs need an object. They are **transitive**. Some verbs don't need an object. They are **intransitive**. This information is important for making good sentences. Look for the symbol [**T**] or [**I**].

Some words can be spelt in **British** English (e.g., *colour, centre*) or **American** English (e.g., *color, center*). Choose the correct spelling for the text you are working on.

Doing reading research

Before you start reading ...

- Think of research questions. In other words, ask yourself: *What must I find out from my research?*

- Look at headings, sub-headings, illustrations. Look for patterns or variations in presentation, e.g., a series of dates; words in **bold** or *italic* script. Think: *What information do they give me?*

- Decide how to record information from your reading. Choose one or more methods of note-taking. **See Unit 1 *Skills bank***

While you are reading ...

- Highlight the topic sentences.

- Think: *Which paragraph(s) will probably give me the answer to my research questions?*

- Read these paragraph(s) first.

- Make notes.

After reading ...

- Think: *Did the text answer all my research questions?*

- If the answer is no, look at other paragraphs to see if the information is there.

Using topic sentences to summarize

The topic sentences of a text normally make a good basis for a summary. Follow this procedure:

- Locate the topic sentences.

- Paraphrase them – in other words, rewrite them in your own words so that the meaning is the same. Do not simply copy them. (This is a form of plagiarism.)

- Add supporting information – once again, in your own words.

Example:

Topic sentence	*When ICT first appeared in the workplace, many people feared they would lose their jobs to machines.*
Paraphrase of topic sentence	*The introduction of ICT in the workplace caused many employees to fear that they would be replaced by machines.*
Supporting information and examples (summarized)	*Many people have had to learn new skills so that they can find jobs in computer-related fields ... Some people now have more interesting jobs ...*

- Check your summary. Check that the ideas flow logically. Check spelling and grammar. If your summary is short, it may be just one paragraph. For a longer summary, divide it into paragraphs.

3 INTRODUCTION TO ICT SYSTEMS

3.1 Vocabulary   stress within words • prefixes

A Discuss these questions.

1 When do you use ICT or see ICT being used around you in your everyday life?
2 What are the benefits of ICT to your life?
3 Are there any disadvantages?

B Study the pictures on the opposite page.

1 What aspects of life do they show? Talk about each picture using words from box a. (You will not need all the words.)
2 How does each item work?

> **a** alarm application automated biometric control device global machine monitoring online passport positioning protocol receiver remote system teller wireless

C Look at the words in box a.

1 Underline the stressed syllable in each word.
2 Which of these words has the same stress pattern as *global*?
3 Sort the other words into groups according to their stress patterns.

D Complete each sentence with a word from box a. Change the form if necessary.

1 The _____ system went off when someone tried to break into the house.
2 You need a personal identification number (PIN) to take money out of the _____ teller machine.
3 The microchip in a biometric _____ contains information about an individual, such as their fingerprints or a face scan.
4 _____ shopping is a convenient way to buy things, but many people worry about Internet fraud.
5 Global _____ systems use signals from satellites to triangulate their position. This information can then be displayed in map form to help drivers travel from one place to another.
6 Use the remote _____ to select the channel you want to watch.
7 Body function _____ devices give information which doctors can use to treat a patient's condition.
8 WAP phones use wireless _____ protocol.

E Study the words in box b. Find the prefix and try to work out the meaning in each case.

> **b**
> | automated | binary | embed | output | predecessor |
> | automation | bidirectional | encode | outsource | preformat |
> | automaton | biannual | enable | outline | preprogram |

F Complete each sentence with a word from box b. Change the form if necessary.

1 Manufacturing processes which are controlled by computers are said to be _____ .
2 A _____ system uses only two numbers, '1' and '0'.
3 Laser printers and VDU screens are examples of _____ devices.
4 The latest computers are much faster than their _____ .
5 Most of today's washing machines have _____ ICT systems.

A Study the handout on the right from a lecture about ICT systems.

  1 What do you expect to hear in the lecture? Make a list of points.

  2 Write down some key words you expect to hear.

  3 Check the pronunciation of the key words, with other students or with a dictionary.

  4 How are you going to prepare for this lecture?

B 🎧 Listen to Part 1 of the lecture.

  1 What exactly is the lecturer going to talk about today? Tick the topic(s) you heard.

    • how people use ICT systems   ____

    • communications systems   ✓

    • what ICT systems are   ✓

    • what ICT systems do   ✓

    • different types of computers   ✓

  2 What does the lecturer give definitions of?

  3 What is a good way to organize notes for this lecture?

C 🎧 Listen to Part 2 of the lecture.

  1 What is the main idea of this section?

  2 What example of an *information system* does the lecturer give?

  3 What does a *control system* do?

  4 What three examples of *communication channels* does the lecturer mention?

  5 What do you expect to hear in the next part of the lecture?

D 🎧 Listen to Part 3 of the lecture.

  1 How could you write notes for this part?

  2 What two components of ICT systems are discussed and what are their definitions?

E 🎧 Listen to Part 4 of the lecture.

  1 Check your definitions of the two components.

  2 What is the research task?

F 🎧 Listen and say whether these sentences are true or false according to the lecture.

  1 _F_   **2** _F_   **3** _T_   **4** _F_   **5** _F_   **6** _F_

G Look at the pictures in the Hadford University lecture handout.

  1 What does each picture show?

  2 Ask and answer questions about each item.

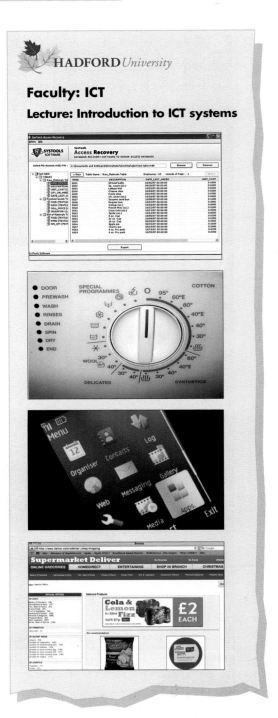

HADFORD *University*

Faculty: ICT

Lecture: Introduction to ICT systems

3.3 Extending skills

stress within words • using information sources • reporting research findings

A 🎧 Listen to some stressed syllables. Identify the word below in each case. Number each word.

Example:

You hear: *1 lec* /lek/   You write:

application	16	database	11	management	2
automated	13	electrical	1	process	10
binary	6	embedded	9	regulate	15
communicate	3	function	14	satellite	12
component	4	information	8	storage	5
control	7	instruction	17	system	18

B Where is the stress in each multi-syllable word in Exercise A?

   1 Mark the stress.

   2 Practise saying each word.

C Work in pairs or groups. Define one of the words in Exercise A. The other student(s) must find and say the correct word.

D Look at the items in the photos on the right.

   1 Decide whether the ICT systems shown are input devices (I), output devices (O) or storage devices (S).

   2 Say what each item is used for.

   3 How many other items can you add to each of the three categories?

Item	I/O/S	Use?
1 Flash drive	S	Portable memory device

E Before you attend a lecture you should do some research.

   1 How could you research the lecture topics on the right?

   2 What information should you record?

   3 How could you record the information?

F You are going to do some research on a particular lecture topic. You must find:

   1 a dictionary definition

   2 an encyclopedia explanation

   3 a useful Internet site

HADFORD *University*

Faculty: ICT

   1   Encoding data

   2   Microprocessors: a brief history

   3   Data processing

   4   Computers of the future: quantum computing

Student A

• Do some research on **encoding data**.

• Tell your partner about your findings.

Student B

• Do some research on **data processing**.

• Tell your partner about your findings.

A You are going to listen to a continuation of the lecture in Lesson 3.2.
  1 Make a list of points from that lecture.
  2 What is the lecturer going to talk about today? (Clue: Lesson 3.2. research task)
  3 🎧 Listen to the end of the last lecture again and check your ideas.
  4 Report your findings from the research task in Lesson 3.3, Exercise F.

B Look at the slides for today's lecture on the opposite page.
  1 What is shown in Slide 1?
  2 What is shown in Slides 2 and 3?
  3 What does the system in Slides 2 and 3 do?

C 🎧 Listen to Part 1 of today's lecture.
  1 What are the three stages that data goes through?
  2 What is the difference between *data* and *information*?
  3 What is the best way to make notes from this lecture? Prepare a page in your notebook.

D 🎧 Listen to Part 2 of the lecture. Make notes. If necessary, ask other students for information.

E What is the lecturer going to talk about next?
  1 🎧 Listen to the beginning of Part 3 and check your ideas.
  2 🎧 Now listen to the rest of the lecture. Make notes. If necessary, ask other students for information.

F Match the words and definitions.
  1 device ☐
  2 instruction ☐
  3 decode ☐
  4 transmit ☐
  5 control (v) ☐
  6 component ☐
  7 cycle ☐
  8 system *b*

  a move information from one place to another
  b a set of connected devices which work together
  c one of a number of parts that form something bigger
  d a continuous process with no beginning or end
  e an order to do something
  f regulate or instruct something
  g change from a coded form to a recognizable form
  h an object invented to perform a function

G Draw and label a simple diagram of a control system cycle. Working with a partner, explain your diagram, using some words and definitions from Exercise F.

H Think of a word from this unit for each definition in the blue box.

> a binary digit   information without a context   change information into data
> a small device which acts on input data

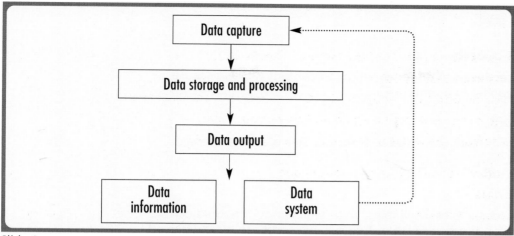

Slide 1

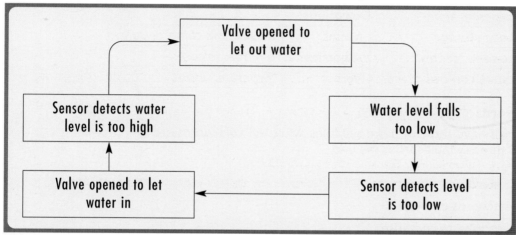

Slide 2

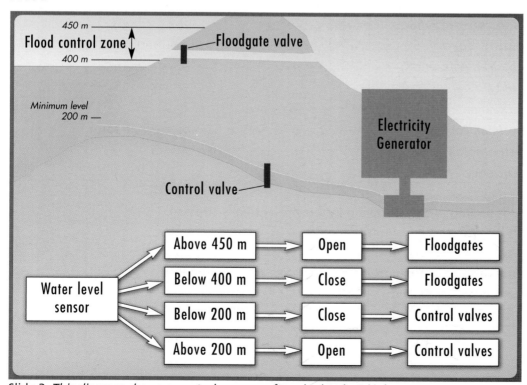

Slide 3 *This diagram shows a control program for a hydroelectric dam.*

Stress within words

Nouns, verbs, adjectives and **adverbs** are called **content words** because they carry the meaning in a sentence.

One-syllable words

Some content words have **one syllable** or sound. This is always stressed.

Examples: 'screen, 'text, 'mouse

Two-syllable words

Some content words have **two syllables**. Two-syllable nouns and adjectives are often stressed on the first syllable. Two-syllable verbs are often stressed on the second syllable.

Examples:

Nouns	'data, 'storage
Adjectives	'modern, 'central
Verbs	in'stall, con'trol

Exceptions:

Nouns	de'vice, ma'chine, re'sult
Adjectives	u'nique, se'cure
Verbs	'program, 'input

Multi-syllable words

Some content words have **three or more syllables**. Multi-syllable words are normally stressed three syllables from the end.

Example:

O o o ⠀ o O o o ⠀ o o O o o

This is true for most words ending in:

~ize/~ise	'authorize, 'summarise
~sis	a'nalysis
~ate	'automate, 'regulate
~ify	'classify, 'specify
~ical	'physical, nu'merical
~ity	u'tility, a'bility
~ular	par'ticular, 'regular
~al	'decimal, con'tinual
~ology	metho'dology
~cy	e'fficiency

Exceptions:
Multi-syllable words ending in the following letters are normally stressed two syllables from the end.

~ic	auto'matic, bio'metric
~ion	appli'cation, con'version
~ent	com'ponent, e'fficient
~tial	diffe'rential

Getting information from other people

From the lecturer

We can sometimes ask a lecturer questions at the end of a lecture. Introduce each question in a polite or tentative way.

Examples:
Could you go over the bit about data storage *again*?
I didn't quite understand what you said about encoding data.
I wonder if you could repeat the four hardware components, please.
Would you mind giving the definition of an embedded system *again*?

From other students

It is a good idea to ask other students after a lecture for information to complete your notes.

Examples:
What did the lecturer say about applications software?
Why did she say that ICT systems can be embedded or general purpose?
I didn't get the bit about the difference between systems software and applications software.

Be polite!

It sometimes sounds impolite to ask people a direct question. We often add a polite introduction.

Examples:
How do computers store data?
➔ (polite) *Do you know how* computers store data?

What does 'encode' mean?
➔ (polite) *Can you remember what* 'encode' means?

What is trilateration?
➔ (polite) *Could you tell me something about* 'trilateration'?

Reporting information to other people

We often have to report research findings to a tutor or other students in a seminar. Make sure you can give:

- sources – books, articles, writers, publication dates
- quotes – in the writer's own words
- summary findings – in your own words

A Study the words and phrases in box a.

1 Which words or phrases relate to ICT? Which relate to books and libraries? Find two groups of words.

2 Find pairs of words and phrases with similar meanings, one from each group.

3 Check your ideas with the first part of *The Computer Jargon Buster* on the opposite page.

B Complete the instructions for using the Learning Resource Centre with words or phrases from box a.

C Study the abbreviations and acronyms in box b.

1 How do you say each one?

2 Divide them into two groups:

• abbreviations

• acronyms

See *Vocabulary bank*

D Test each other on the items in Exercise C.

1 What do the letters stand for in each case?

2 What do they mean?

3 Check your ideas with the second part of *The Computer Jargon Buster* on the opposite page.

E Study the nouns in box c.

1 Make a verb from each noun.

2 Make another noun from the verb.

---

a

books   browse/search   catalogue
close   cross-reference   database
electronic resources   exit/log off   hyperlink
index   library   log in/log on   look up
menu   open   page   search engine
table of contents   web page   World Wide Web

HADFORD *University*

Learning Resource Centre

Instructions for use:
If you want to access web pages on the
_____ , you must first
_____ to the university intranet
with your username and password. You
can use any _____ but the
default is Google. _____ for web
pages by typing one or more keywords in
the search box and clicking on **Search**, or
pressing **Enter**. When the results appear,
click on a _____ (highlighted in
blue) to jump to the web page. Click on
Back to return to the results listing.
You can also use the university
_____ of learning resources.
Click on **ICT Resources** on the main
_____ .

---

b

CAL   CLI   GUI   HCI   HTML
HTTP   ISP   RAM   ROM   URL
USB   VLE   WIMP   WWW

---

c

class   computer   digit
identity   machine

Computer Weekly International Magazine

The Computer Jargon Buster

There are many common words used about books and libraries which are translated into jargon words when we talk about using computers and the Internet for similar functions.

books	electronic resources
index	search engine
cross-reference	hyperlink
catalogue	database
library	World Wide Web
table of contents	menu
look up	browse/search
page	web page
open	log in/log on
close	exit/log off

There are many abbreviations and acronyms in computing. Learn some useful ones.

Abbr./Acr.	What it stands for	What it means
CAL	computer-assisted learning	using computers to help you learn
CLI	command line interface	a way to interact with a computer using lines of text
GUI	graphical user interface	a way to interact with a computer using a mouse to point and click on images
HCI	human-computer interaction	the way that a user works with a computer system
HTML	hypertext markup language	a way to write documents so they can be displayed on a website
HTTP	hypertext transfer protocol	a set of rules for transfering files on the WWW, usually included at the beginning of a website address (e.g., http://www. ...)
ISP	Internet service provider	a company that enables access to the Internet
RAM	random-access memory	the memory you can use to store your own information
ROM	read-only memory	a type of permanent computer or disk memory that stores information that can be read or used but not changed
URL	uniform resource locator	a website address, e.g., http://www.garneteducation.com
USB	universal serial bus	a standard way to connect things like printers and scanners to a computer
VLE	virtual learning environment	a software program for computerized learning
WIMP	windows, icons, menus, pointers	a way to interact with a computer using windows, icons, menus and pointing devices (see GUI)
WWW	World Wide Web	a huge collection of documents that are connected by hypertext links and can be accessed through the Internet

A Discuss these questions.

 1 How are computers used in education today?

 2 What are the advantages of using computers for learning?

B Look at the title of the text on the opposite page.

 1 What does 'computer-assisted learning' mean?

 2 What sort of courses can CAL be used in? Make a list.

 3 Write some questions that you would like the text to answer.

C Work in pairs. Look at the diagram on this page.

 1 Describe it.

 2 What sort of things do you think each component includes?

D One student wrote some ideas about CAL before reading the text on the opposite page. Write **A** (I agree), **D** (I disagree) or **?** (I'm not sure) next to the ideas on the right.

E Look carefully at the topic sentences in the text on the opposite page.

 1 Identify the topic and comment about the topic. See *Skills bank*

 2 What do you think each paragraph will be about?

F Read the text carefully. Were your questions from Exercise B answered?

G Does the writer of the text agree or disagree with the ideas in Exercise D? Which ideas are not mentioned?

H Study the notes a student made in the margin of the text on the opposite page.

 1 What ideas are in the other paragraphs? Write some key words.

 2 Which words introduce new ideas in each paragraph? See *Skills bank*

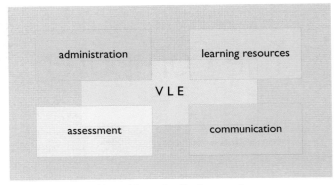

Virtual Learning Environment

CAL has always been easy to use. ____

Teachers didn't like using CAL software products at first. ____

CAL is just another addition to traditional teaching methods. ____

CAL has radically changed the way people learn. ____

In the future, teachers will be replaced by CAL. ____

HADFORD *University*

Computer-Assisted Learning

Computers in education

Early probs.

Improvement and investment

Computers have been used in education since the 1960s. Initially, they tended to only be used in computer-related subjects because they were, unfortunately, quite difficult to use. This was because they had command line interfaces (CLI). Users had to type long lines of text in order to get the computer to do something. However, the 1980s saw the advent of the first graphical user interfaces (GUIs) which were much more user-friendly. This improvement in human-computer interaction (HCI), together with new subject-specific software, made it viable to employ computers in more subjects. Education institutions began to see the value of computer-assisted learning (CAL). Many invested heavily in equipment and training, the outcome of which can be seen today in many classrooms around the world.

By the end of the 20th century, there was a whole range of CAL software products on offer. In general, the first CAL programs were not terribly exciting. However, in the late 1980s, CD-ROMs and other multimedia products became available. These made it possible to produce software with sound and graphics which was also easy to distribute. As a result, more businesses became involved in developing educational software. The new products were attractive and many students enjoyed using them. Nevertheless, they were expensive. In addition, they were often perceived to be just a different way of learning or testing the same things. Teachers who disliked using computers were largely able to ignore them or confine them to self-study.

By contrast, it was difficult to ignore the arrival of the Internet, which heralded a new phase in CAL and had a huge impact on education. Although slow links and download times characterized the early days of the Internet, the development of broadband technology provided much speedier access. The Internet provides an alternative to textbook-based learning and access to authentic, up-to-date online resources. Furthermore, it offers students a way to communicate with each other, and with the outside world. They can even publish their work on the Web for others. Now CAL is more than a 'bolt-on' to traditional teaching. It requires new skills, such as the ability to find information, evaluate websites, or to collaborate with others via a network.

Effect of CAL on way of learning

Benefits of VLE

CAL not only influences *how* and *what* students learn; it also affects *where* they learn. Many courses now incorporate a virtual learning environment (VLE), which is a set of computer-based teaching and learning tools used to teach distance-learning programmes or to support face-to-face courses. VLEs are similar to websites in many ways. Like websites, they run on a server and can be accessed via an Internet connection. VLEs contain a number of components which, typically, would include the following. Firstly, there is an administrative element providing course information, such as student tasks and how to get help. Secondly, there are the learning resources used to deliver the course, including materials designed by the teacher, or links to sources of information. Thirdly, there is a range of assessment tools which can be used to chart progress during the course. VLEs also have communication tools, such as e-mail, for students to contact, or correspond with, their teachers or their peers.

Clearly, CAL is set to play an important role in education in the future. Some people even believe that it will eventually replace the need for teachers or classrooms. However, it is more likely that VLEs are the future of computer-assisted learning. This means that subject teachers are faced with a new challenge. They will not only need to be experts in their field, for example history or French, but they will also have to become confident users of new technology.

A Discuss these questions.

  1 You want to find out about computers in teaching and learning. Where would you look for the information? Why?

  2 What keywords would you use to make this search? Why?

B Your search produces 50 results. How can you select the most useful ones without reading all of them? Look at the list of criteria on the right and put a tick or '?'.

C You want to research the following. Choose up to three keywords or phrases for each search.

  1 invention of World Wide Web

  2 types of communication tools found in a VLE

  3 where to find online learning activities for ICT

D Go to a computer and try out your chosen keywords.

> Criteria for choosing to read a result
>
> It contains all of my keywords. ____
> The document comes from a journal. ____
> It is in the first ten. ____
> It has this year's date. ____
> It is a large document. ____
> The website address ends in .org ____
> The website address ends in .edu ____
> The website address contains .ac ____
> It is a PDF file. ____
> It refers to ICT. ____
> It refers to a person I don't know. ____
> It refers to an organization I know. ____

A What information is contained in the results listing of a search engine?

  1 Make a list.

  2 Check with the results listing on the opposite page.

B Scan the results listings. Answer these questions.

  1 What keywords were entered?

  2 Why was *journal* used as a keyword? Why is it not in inverted commas?

C Answer these questions.

  1 Which results contain abbreviations or acronyms?

  2 Where is the website address in each result?

  3 Which are PDF documents?

  4 What do the different coloured fonts represent?

  5 Which results refer to journals?

  6 Which results refer to educational institutions?

  7 Which results are commercial sites?

  8 Which country does result 7 come from?

  9 What does *similar pages* mean?

  10 What does *cached* mean?

D Continue your research on computer-assisted learning by entering the keywords into a search engine and accessing three of the results.

  1 Make notes.

  2 Compare your findings with other students.

E Choose the most interesting result. Write a paragraph about the information you discovered. Develop the topic within the paragraph with discourse markers and stance markers.

Google

Sign in

Web   Images   Groups   News   Froogle   Maps   **more »**

Search   Advanced Search
Preferences

Web   Results **1 - 10** of about **289** for "Computer assisted learning" + journal + "latest technology"

1 Journal of Computer Assisted Learning-Vol 26. Issue 5 …
The **Journal** of **Computer Assisted Learning** is a quarterly, peer-reviewed, international journal which covers the whole range of users of information and communication **technology** to support learning and knowledge exchange.
http://onlinelibrary.wiley.com/journal/10.1111/%28ISSN%291365-2729 - Cached

2 An evaluation of computer-assisted learning in mathematics …
11 Jul 2010 – An evaluation of **computer-assisted learning** in mathematics … International Journal of Mathematical Education in Science and **Technology,** Vol 23
www.informaworld.com/…/content~content=a746869072 - Cached

3 JOLT – Journal of Online Learning and Teaching
15 Dec 2009 – A USB dongle similar to a flash drive serves as the wireless receiver … , Journal of **Computer Assisted Learning**, 20(2), 81-94. doi: 10.1111/j.1365-2729.2004.00074 … Journal of Research on **Technology** in Education, 41(2), 161-177. …
jolt.merlot.org/vol5no4/klein_1209.htm - Cached - Similar

4 E-Learning Journals
30 Jun 2010 – Journals with a focus on English Studies and **Technology** … Published three times per year, the magazine contains in-depth articles on the latest learning trends and developments as well as … **Journal** of **Computer-Assisted Learning** …
www.english.heacademy.ac.uk/…/technology/journals.php - Cached - Similar*

5 [PDF] Teaching Computer Science in Higher Education: Enabling Learning …
24 Jun 2010 – More than just the latest technology buzzword, it's a transformative force that's … in multimedia **Computer** Aided **Learning. Journal** (CALJ) …
fie-conference.org/fie2010/papers/1100.pdf - Cached - Similar

6 Learning interaction and networked communities
20 Jul 2010 – A current focus is on designing technologies that incorporate learning interaction and dialogue design. Paper in Proceedings of International Workshop on Learning Interaction and **Learning Technology.**
www.londonmet.ac.uk/ltri/research/interaction.htm - Cached - Similar

7 AJET: Australasian Journal of Educational Technology
15 Mar 2010 – articles in educational **technology,** educational design, multimedia, **computer assisted learning,** and related areas. AJET is published by the Australasian Society for Computers in Learning in Tertiary Education (ASCILITE) …
www.ascilite.org.au/ajet/about/about.html - Cached - Similar

8 [PDF] LEARNING AND TEACHING AWARDS
15 Feb 2010 – **Technology**-enhanced **learning,** or **computer** aided **learning** (e-learning) can be institutionally … assisted teaching sessions. Figure 3 explains the process of learning for all three … the **latest technology** and e-learning packages which … establishing criteria for e-learning development.
www.becta.org.uk/page_documents/research/ictres_update02_04.pdf - Similar pages

9 Promoting computer assisted learning for persons with disabilities …
6 May 2010 – The current **technologies** allow computer applications with a higher degree of accessibility … **Computer Assisted Learning** (CAL) solutions for people with visual disabilities. A basis of many accessible tools for …
linkinghub.elsevier.com/retrieve/pii/S1877042810007597 - Cached - Similar

10 'CAL'– Past, present and beyond - Crook - 2010 - Journal of Computer Assisted Learning …
… 2002) nor to regard the latest **technology** as a replacement for more traditional … and distance **learning, Journal** of **Computer Assisted Learning,** Vol. …
onlinelibrary.wiley.com/doi/10.1111/j.1365-2729.2009.00343.x/full - Similar pages

*Note that this link refers to an institution that will no longer be funded from July 2011, so link is likely to become inactive.

Understanding abbreviations and acronyms

An **abbreviation** is a shorter version of something. For example, PC /piːsiː/ is an abbreviation for *personal computer*.

An **acronym** is similar to an abbreviation, but it is pronounced as a word. For example, CAL /kæl/ is an acronym for *computer-assisted learning*.

We normally write an abbreviation or acronym with **capital letters**, although the full words have lower case letters. However, there are exceptions, such as www, which is often written with lower case letters.

We **pronounce** the vowel letters in **abbreviations** in this way:

A	/eɪ/
E	/iː/
I	/aɪ/
O	/əʊ/
U	/juː/

We normally **pronounce** the vowel letters in **acronyms** in this way:

A	/æ/
E	/e/
I	/ɪ/
O	/ɒ/
U	/ʌ/

Common suffixes

Suffixes for verbs

There are some common verb suffixes. They make nouns into verbs. The meaning is basically *make* + noun.

Examples:

~ize	computerize, mechanize, digitize
~(i)fy	classify, specify, modify
~ate	navigate, communicate, innovate
~en	broaden, lengthen, strengthen

Suffixes for nouns

Many nouns are made by adding a suffix to a verb. This means:
- You can identify many nouns from a suffix.
- You can often discover the verb by removing the suffix.

Sometimes you have to make changes to the end of the verb.

Examples:

Verb	Suffix	Noun
produce	+ tion	production
perform	+ nce	performance
computerize*	+ tion	computerization
manufacture	+ ing	manufacturing
coordinate	+ ion	coordination
specify	+ ication	specification

*both ~ise/~ize (~isation/~ization) forms are acceptable in British English. American English usage is ~ize (~ization).

Developing ideas in a paragraph

Introducing the topic

In a text, **a new paragraph** indicates the start of **a new topic**.

The topic is given in the **topic sentence**, which is at or near the beginning of the paragraph. The topic sentence gives the topic, and also makes a comment about the topic.

Example:
By contrast, it was difficult to ignore the arrival of the Internet, which heralded a new phase in CAL.

The **topic** is *the Internet*. The **comment** is that this *heralded a new phase in CAL*. The sentences that follow then expand or explain the topic sentence.

Examples:
It has had a huge impact on education … The Internet provides an alternative to textbook learning … It offers students a way to communicate … Now CAL is more than a 'bolt on' to traditional teaching … It requires new skills …

Developing the topic

A paragraph is normally about the same basic topic (the 'unity' principle). However, within a paragraph, ideas often **develop** beyond the initial comment. This development is often shown by
- **a discourse marker**: *but, however*, etc.
- **a stance marker**: *unfortunately*, etc.

Examples:
***However**, the 1980s saw the advent of the first graphical user interfaces (GUIs). These were much more user-friendly.*

*Slow links and download times characterized the early days of the Internet. **Thankfully**, however, broadband technology soon changed this.*

Discourse markers generally make a connection between the previous information and what comes next. They mainly introduce **contrasts** or **additional information**.

Stance markers show the **attitude** of the writer to the information, i.e., whether he/she is surprised, pleased, unhappy, etc. about the information.

Recording and reporting findings

When you do your research, record information about the source. Refer to the source when you report your findings.

Examples:
Tim Berners-Lee (2007) states that …
As Aydin, Harmsen, van Slooten & Stegwee suggest in their 2005 article in *The Journal of Database Management, …*
According to Brooks in his book *The Mythical Man Month and Other Essays on Software Engineering* (1995), …
As the writer of the article on *www.computerweekly.com* (March 29, 2009) says, …

You should give full information about the source in your reference list or bibliography. For more information about this, see Unit 10 ***Skills bank***.

5.1 Vocabulary
word sets: synonyms, antonyms, etc. • describing trends

A Look at the pictures on the opposite page.

1 What do they have in common?

2 Put them in the order of development.

B Study the words in box a.

1 Find pairs of words with similar meanings.

2 What part of speech is each word?

> **a**
>
> architecture   calculate   change   complex
> configure   convert   create   design   develop
> engine   knowledge   machine   precision
> record   set up   sophisticated   stage   step
> store   tolerance   understanding   work out

C Study the Hadford University handout on this page. Find pairs of blue words with similar meanings.

D Study the words in box b.

1 Find pairs of opposites.

2 Group words together to make sets.

3 Try to give a name to each word set.

> **b**
>
> academic   addition   analogue   civilian
> commercial   current   decode   decrypt   digital
> division   encode   encrypt   fixed   flexible
> limited   military   multiplication   multi-purpose
> obsolete   portable   specialized   subtraction

E Work with a partner.

1 Choose an image on the opposite page. Use words from box b to describe it.

2 Your partner should guess which image you are talking about.

F Look at Figure 1.

1 How would you describe the graph?

2 What do each of the lines on the graph show?

G Study the description of Figure 2 on this page. Write one or two words in each space.

HADFORD *University*

Faculty: ICT

Lecture: *The history of computing*

In order to fully understand the current state of the computer, it is essential to know about the key stages in its technical evolution. This introductory lecture will look at these stages, beginning with the abacus – first used to calculate taxes in Babylon in 2500 BCE – and continuing up to the present.

The lecture will examine how, over time, new calculating engines were developed for specific purposes by inventors. It will look at the way in which the architecture of the machines was limited by the tolerance with which parts could be made, using the technology at the time.

The lecture will also explore how machines became more complex as inventors' understanding of computing developed. This includes the kind of machines which had to be configured for each task, as well as machines which were programmable. In addition, it will look at how data was stored and converted into input types suitable for the computer. Finally, it will examine why computers have become necessary in war and how military needs in the 20th century were responsible for so many new developments.

Figure 2 shows changes _____ _____ number and cost of transistors _____ 1971 _____ 1985. Up to 1979, there was a _____ _____ in the number of transistors. During the same period, prices _____ _____. From 1979 to 1985, the cost of the transistors showed a _____ _____. At the same time, the number of transistors _____ _____.

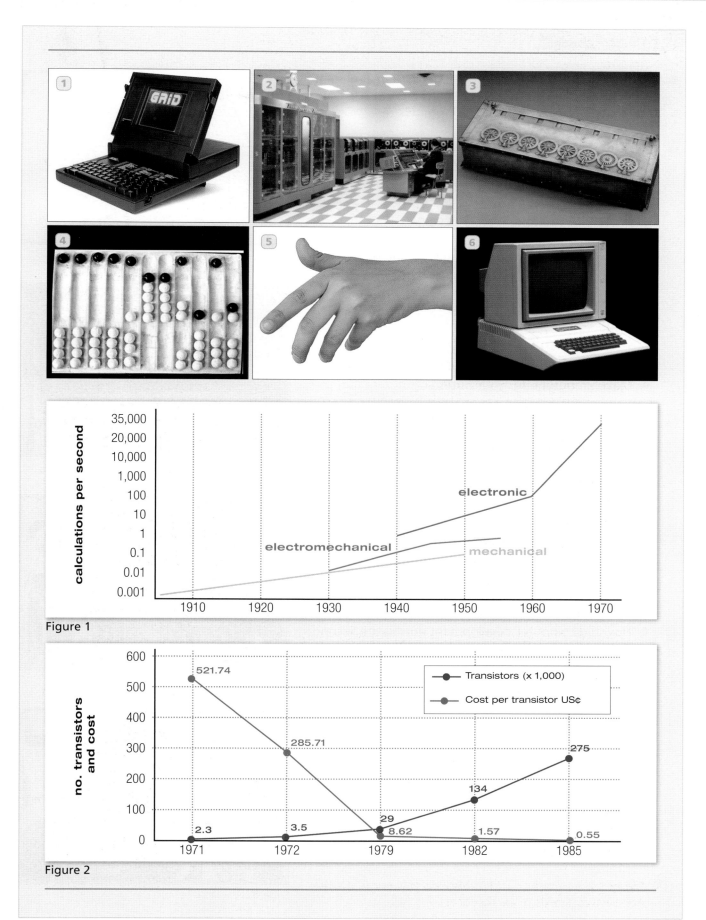

Figure 1

Figure 2

A You are going to hear a lecture about the development of computers. Look at the lecture slides. What will the lecturer talk about? Make a list of points.

B 🎧 Listen to Part 1 of the lecture. How will the lecture be organized? Number these topics.

- computing in the Second World War ____
- mechanical computing ____
- rise of the Internet ____
- pre-mechanical computing ____
- electronic computing ____

C Study the topics in Exercise B.

1 Write some key words for each topic.
2 Can you match the topics with Slides 1–4?
3 What is a good way to make notes?
4 Make an outline for your notes.

D 🎧 Listen to Part 2 of the lecture.

1 Add information to your outline notes.
2 Which of the topics in Exercise B are discussed? In what order?
3 Why was the Jacquard Loom important?

E 🎧 Listen to Part 3 of the lecture. Make notes.

1 Which topics in Exercise B are discussed?
2 Which topic has not been mentioned?
3 What challenge helped computers develop in the late 19th century?
4 How did computer development during the Second World War move technology forward?

F The lecturer used these words and phrases. Match synonyms.

1	key concept	a	calculating
2	adding	b	do
3	important people	c	machine
4	jump ahead	d	important point
5	perform	e	key figures
6	invented	f	move forward
7	device	g	created

Slide 1

Slide 2

Slide 3

Slide 4

5.3 Extending skills
note-taking symbols • stress within words • lecture language

A Look at the student notes on the right. They are from the lecture in Lesson 5.2.

1 What do the symbols and abbreviations mean?

2 The notes contain some mistakes. Find and correct them.

3 Make the corrected notes into a spidergram.

B 🎧 Listen to the final part of the lecture.

1 Complete your notes.

2 Why does the lecture have to stop?

3 What is the research task?

C 🎧 Listen to some stressed syllables. Identify the word below in each case. Number each word.

Example: You hear: *1 crypt* /krɪpt/

You write:

arithmetic ____   chip ____   digital ____   programmability ____

addition ____   computation ____   magnetic ____   subtraction ____

calculation ____   cryptography *1*   mechanical ____   transistor ____

D Study the extract from the lecture on the right.

1 Think of one word for each space.

2 🎧 Listen and check your ideas.

3 Match words or phrases from the blue box below with each word or phrase from the lecture.

4 Think of other words or phrases with similar meanings.

> basically   by that I mean   for example
> for instance   in fact   possibly   probably
> some people say   that is to say
> to put it another way   we can see that
> we won't spend too much time on this

E Discuss the research task set by the lecturer.

1 What kind of information should you find?

2 What do you already know?

3 Where can you find more information?

Mechanical computing

(i) Hollerith – late C19ᵗʰ, tabulating machines using gears & paper tape. Used US Census 1880 and ↓ time by 7 yrs. Company became IBM.

(ii) 1932 – Bush (MIT) – Differential Analyzer comm. use = elec. motors & gears, binary

WW2

(iii) WW2 – UK, Turing broke German code using Colossus = 1st electronic computer, analogue, used valves + relays. Innovative, e.g., punched card input, enormous impact on war.

The computer is _____ the most important piece of technology in modern society, but it _____ has a very long history, in fact going back almost 5,000 years. It starts with the early Babylonians, who used simple arithmetic to count and keep a record of their goods.

As their wealth grew and they had more and more goods to record, *it* _____ *that* they would try to develop tools to make this work easier.

A *good* _____ *of* one of these tools is the abacus, used as a basic calculator – *in* _____ *words*, a computer. *What I* _____ *is that*, as in a computer, data is input by moving the beads. It is stored by the position of the beads and the output or answers can then be read off. Five beads per line are often used, just as there are five fingers on a hand. _____ , *moving* _____ to the early 17th century, we find a different type of computer.

A Study the graph on the opposite page.

   1 What does it show?

   2 What is the connection between the graph and the development of the Internet?

B 🎧 Listen to some extracts from a seminar about the creation of the Internet.

   1 What is wrong with the contribution of the last speaker in each case? Choose from the following:

     • it is irrelevant

     • the student interrupts

     • the student doesn't contribute anything to the discussion

     • it is not polite

     • it is relevant but the student doesn't explain the relevance

   2 What exactly does the student say, in each case?

   3 What should the student say or do, in each case?

C 🎧 Listen to some more extracts from the same seminar.

   1 How does the second speaker make an effective contribution in each case? Choose from the following:
He/she …

     • asks for clarification

     • paraphrases to check understanding

     • brings the discussion back to the main point

     • disagrees politely with a previous speaker

     • brings in another speaker

     • gives specific examples to help explain a point

   2 What exactly does the student say, in each case?

   3 What other ways do you know of saying the same things?

D Make a table of **Do's** (helpful ways) and **Don't**s (unhelpful ways) of contributing to seminar discussions.

Do's	Don'ts
ask politely for information	demand information from other students

E Work in groups.

   1 Look at the pictures on the opposite page. Decide which sets of data in Figure 1 the pictures relate to.

   2 Which of the three elements shown in the graph helped contribute most to speeding up the development of the Internet? Look at the graph and make sure you can justify your decisions.

   3 Conduct a seminar. One person should act as observer.

F Report on your discussion and present the feedback from your group, giving reasons for your decisions.

G Work in groups of four. Each person should research and discuss one of the four main types of research. The teacher will give you a *discussion task card* with more instructions.

     • Student A: find out about *secondary research* (information on page 102)

     • Student B: find out about *primary research* (information on page 102)

     • Student C: find out about *quantitative research* (information on page 105)

     • Student D: find out about *qualitative research* (information on page 106)

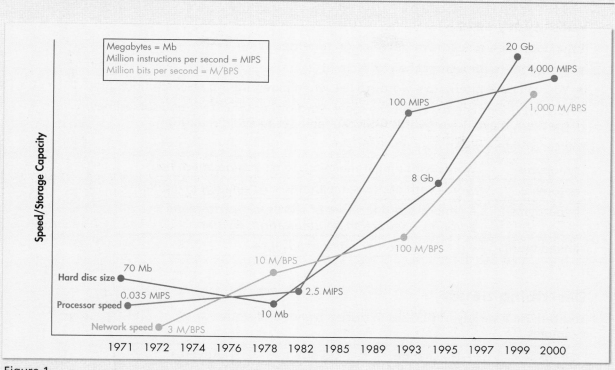

Figure 1

Vocabulary sets

It is a good idea to learn words which go together. Why?

- It is easier to remember the words.
- You will have alternative words to use when paraphrasing research findings.
- It is not good style to repeat the same word often, so writers, and sometimes speakers, make use of words from the same set to avoid repetition.

You can create a vocabulary set with:

synonyms	words with similar meanings, e.g., *engine, machine*
antonyms	words with opposite meanings, e.g., *analogue, digital*
hypernyms	a general word for a set of words, e.g., *arithmetic = addition, subtraction, multiplication, division*
linked words	e.g., *innovation, invention, advance*

Describing trends

You can use a variety of phrases to discuss trends and statistics.
Examples:

Go up	No change	Go down	Adverbs
rise *increase* *grow* *improve* *soar*	*stay the same* *remain at …* *doesn't change* *is unchanged*	*fall* *decrease* *decline* *worsen* *drop* *plunge* *plummet*	*slightly* *gradually* *steadily* *significantly* *sharply* *dramatically*

Stance

Speakers often use certain words and phrases to show how they feel about what they are saying. Common stance words are:

adverbs	*arguably* *naturally* *unfortunately*
phrases	*of course, …* *it's essential to/that …* *we might say that …*

In many cases, different stance words and phrases are used in spoken and written language.

Spoken	Written
another thing	*additionally*
it seems	*evidently*
unfortunately	*regrettably*
believe	*contend*

Signpost language in a lecture

At the beginning of a lecture, a speaker will usually outline the talk. To help listeners understand the order of topics, the speaker will use phrases such as:

To start with I'll talk about …
Then I'll discuss …
After that, we'll look at …
I'll finish by giving a summary of …

During the lecture, the speaker may:

indicate a new topic	*Moving on (from this) …*
say the same thing in a different way	*What I mean is, …* *That is to say, …* *To put it another way, …*
return to the main point	*Where was I? Oh, yes.* *To return to the main point …* *As I was saying …*

Seminar language

The discussion leader may:

ask for information	*What did you learn about …?* *Can you explain …?* *Can you tell me a bit more about …?*
ask for opinions	*What do you make of …?* *This is interesting, isn't it?*
bring in other speakers	*What do you think, Majed?* *What's your opinion, Evie?*

Participants should:

be polite when disagreeing	*Actually, I don't quite agree …*
make relevant contributions	*That reminds me …*
give examples to explain a point	*I can give an example of that.*

Participants may:

agree with previous speaker	*I agree, and that's why …* *That's true, so I think …* *You're absolutely right, which is why …*
disagree with previous speaker	*I don't think I agree with that. In my opinion …* *I'm not sure that's true. I think …*
link to a previous speaker	*As Jack said earlier …* *Going back to what Leila said a while ago …*
ask for clarification	*Could you say more about …?*
paraphrase to check understanding	*So what you're saying is …*
refer back to establish relevance	*Just going back to …*

Participants may not be sure if a contribution is new or relevant:
I'm sorry. Has anybody made the point that …?
I don't know if this is relevant but …

6.1 Vocabulary   paraphrasing at sentence level

A Study the words in the blue box.

1 Copy and complete the table. Put the words in one or more boxes, in each case.

2 Add affixes to make words for the empty boxes. (Some will not be possible.)

3 What is the special meaning of each word in relation to the Internet?

4 Find a synonym for each word in the blue box.

5 Group the words in the blue box according to their stress pattern.

B Study Figure 1 on the opposite page. Discuss these questions using words from Exercise A.

1 What do the screenshots show?

2 What are the similarities and differences between the two images?

C Study Figure 2 on the opposite page.

1 What does the graph show?

2 What connection is there between Figure 1 and Figure 2?

3 What use could be made of the data for each of the protocols?

D Student A has written about changes in data transfers over the Internet, but there are some mistakes. Change the blue words, so the sentences are true.

E Student B has also written about changes in data transfers over the Internet. Match each sentence with a corrected sentence from Exercise D.

F Look at Figures 3a and 3b on the opposite page.

1 What do the two diagrams show?

2 Add the missing words to the spaces in 3a and 3b, using words from the blue box and your own knowledge.

3 Write a description of what is happening at each stage, indicated by the number.

4 Identify the similarities and differences between the two diagrams.

---

browser   cache   connection
distribution   host   hypertext
interaction   layer   link   packet
peer   request   response   scale
server   spider   stream   visit

Noun	Verb	Adjective
visit	visit	

Student A

1 The proportion of P2P traffic has risen considerably since 2007.

2 By 2010, data using VoIP protocols was decreasing rapidly.

3 HTTP usage decreased sharply between 2007 and 2009.

4 Gaming has shrunk as a proportion of traffic overall.

5 Streaming more than halved between 2007 and 2010.

6 P2P ceased to be the most common protocol on the Internet in 2010.

Student B

a In 2010, the P2P protocol was still used more than any other protocol on the Internet.

b After 2007, transfers of data using P2P protocols declined significantly.

c The ratio of data using gaming protocols has increased relative to overall traffic on the Internet.

d The proportion of Internet data using streaming protocols in 2009 was over twice as much as it had been in 2007.

e From 2007 to 2009, there was a gradual decline in the use of the HTTP protocol.

f Beginning in 2010, there was rapid growth in VoIP data traffic.

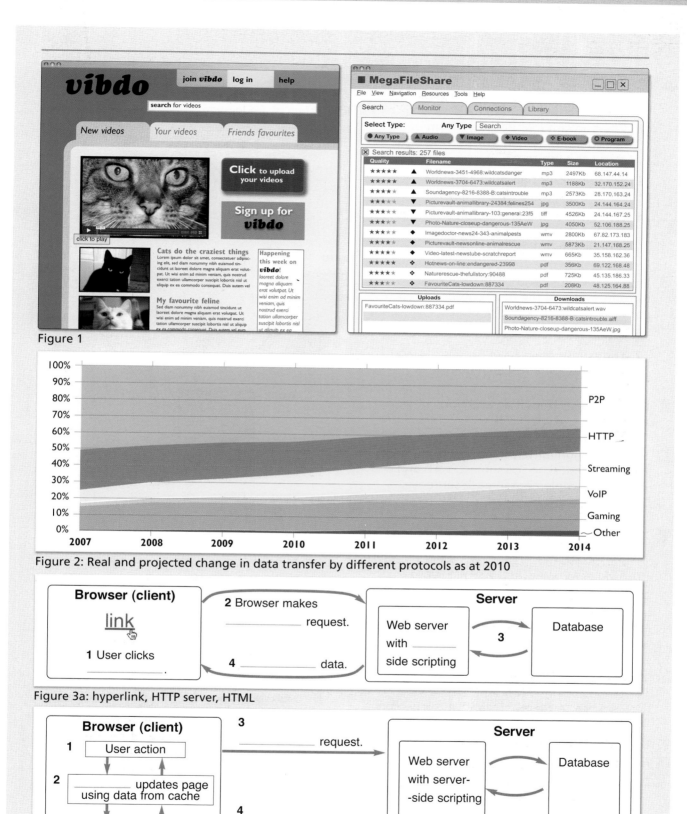

Figure 1

Figure 2: Real and projected change in data transfer by different protocols as at 2010

Figure 3a: hyperlink, HTTP server, HTML

Figure 3b: cache, AJAX, XML, HTTP

A Discuss these questions.

1 What does Figure 1 show?

2 What advantages does this form of network have when transferring data across the Internet?

3 What types of files might people transfer over this type of network?

4 What reasons might there be for the decline in this type of data as a proportion of Internet traffic?

B Look at the illustration, the title, the introduction and the first sentence of each paragraph on the opposite page.

1 What will the text be about?

2 Using your ideas from Exercises A and B1, write some research questions.

C Read the text. Does it answer your questions?

D Study the highlighted sentences in the text. Find and underline the subject, verb and object or complement in each sentence.
See Skills bank

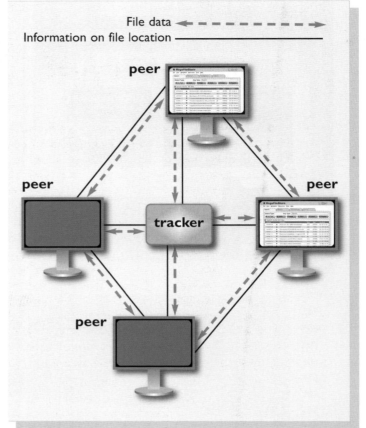

File data
Information on file location

peer
peer   peer
tracker
peer

Figure 1

E Two students paraphrased part of the text.

1 Which part of the text are these paraphrases of?

2 Which paraphrase is better? Why?

Student A

An important Web 2.0 development was that users could now view video and images directly, using their web browser.

Introduced in 1996 as a web-based animation program, Flash ran as a freely available browser plug-in or add-on.

In 2003, when a version of Flash was released which included video streaming, a very high proportion of web users downloaded the plug-in.

The first video was uploaded to YouTube, a web-based video sharing application, in 2005.

Student B

The ability, with Web 2.0, to view pictures and video online, without having to download files, marked a major advance.

Originally introduced in 1996, Flash started out as a free animation program which could be run in a web browser.

When a new release of Flash appeared in 2003, which included video streaming, the plug-in was downloaded by a large number of web users.

YouTube, a web-based application which allowed users to upload and view videos, was launched in 2005.

F Work in groups. Write a paraphrase of a different part of the text.
See Vocabulary bank

Web 2.0:
Real change or hype?

Around the year 2005, a series of radical developments appeared to be changing the way the Internet was used. Large numbers of new online services such as video sharing and social networking were being developed, and huge numbers of people were signing up to use them. For some writers the changes were so significant they used the term 'Web 2.0' to describe them. In software engineering, when a new version of a software package is a huge improvement on the old version, the convention is to add one to the number before the decimal, so that 1.0 becomes 2.0, for example. Where the transition is more gradual, one is added after the decimal. Other writers, however, felt that the term Web 2.0 was unhelpful and the changes were evolutionary rather than revolutionary. So, which view is correct? The best way to analyze Web 2.0 is to identify its key technologies and services. By looking at each service in the context of the developments in web technology which made it possible, we can evaluate the nature of the changes.

The first development we should look at is the creation of *static websites*. Initially, these consisted of mainly text-based web pages, with the occasional image. The pages were written in HyperText Markup Language (HTML), which allowed the writer to vary the size, colour and emphasis of the text, and to include hypertext links to other web pages. Some websites contained forms which allowed users to submit their details, but otherwise the pages were fixed and there was little interactivity. Over time, static websites became bigger, and web pages began to be spidered, indexing the pages so they could be found by search engines. They also began to use more graphics, and to link to document and video files which could be downloaded by users and viewed on desktop applications.

The next stage to consider is the development of *dynamic websites*. These sites used server-side scripting languages to extract data from databases, which was then used to create web pages. One of the most popular languages was PHP (Pre-Hypertext Processor), an open source product. From 1998 onwards, PHP was routinely used with three other open source products – the Linux operating system, Apache web server and MySQL database packages – to power dynamic websites, giving rise to the term *LAMP stack*. Server-side scripting languages made it easy to move data between active web pages and databases, making bulletin boards, blog services and early versions of social networking services possible. Wikipedia, the online encyclopedia, also grew from this technology. However,

these developments were limited by the need to load complete pages each time new data was selected from the database, which made them relatively slow.

It was against this background that Flash and Ajax, the two technologies seen as key to Web 2.0, emerged. A major component of Web 2.0 was the way in which users could directly access visual and audio-visual material in their browser. The first release of Flash was introduced in 1996 as a freely available web-based animation program which would run in a browser plug-in or add-on. The software subsequently went through many incremental changes and became increasingly popular. When a version was released in 2003 which included video streaming, a very high proportion of web browsers had the plug-in installed. Flash fundamentally altered the way in which users could access visual and audio-visual material. Flickr, the online photo album service and YouTube, the video sharing service, which both launched in 2005, were among the first to use and to benefit from the new features of the Flash package. By 2010, Flickr was hosting five billion images and YouTube was serving over two billion videos per day. The other technology associated with Web 2.0 was Ajax (Asynchronous JavaScript and XML), a client-side scripting language which allowed elements of a page to be refreshed without reloading the whole page. This allowed web pages to become almost as interactive as desktop applications.

An important effect of these technologies was on the use of peer-to-peer technologies for accessing audio and video content. Since the late 1990s, users have exchanged music and video files over these networks, much of it copyright material. By making it possible to listen to music and to watch video online, there was less need to download files using P2P in order to share files, and so this type of Internet traffic experienced a drop. However, the fall was gradual and P2P remains popular for higher quality video, games and other materials, as well as in geographical areas with low bandwidth. Although not everyone agrees on how significant technologies such as P2P will continue to be, there is little doubt that the developments associated with Web 2.0 have changed the way we interact online for good.

6.3 Extending skills understanding complex sentences

A Study the words in box a from the text in Lesson 6.2.

1 What part of speech are they in the text?

2 Find a word in the text with a similar meaning to each word.

a

radical version transition
evolutionary development static
dynamic extract product

B Complete the summary with words from Exercise A.

The term Web 2.0 comes from a convention in numbering new software ______________. If ______________ are ______________, the number *after* the decimal is changed. If they are ______________, the number *before* is changed. The development in which websites changed from ______________ to ______________ was very important in the move to Web 2.0. Particularly important were ______________ such as PHP, which could create web pages by ______________ data from databases.

C Study the words in box b.

1 What is each base word and its ICT meaning?

2 How does the affix change the part of speech?

3 What is the meaning in the text in Lesson 6.2?

b

development revolutionary
hypertext interactivity indexing
asynchronous refresh reload

D Study sentences A–E on the opposite page.

1 Copy and complete Table 1. Put the parts of each sentence in the correct column.

2 Rewrite the main part of each sentence, changing the verb from active to passive or vice versa.

E Look at the 'Other verbs' column in Table 1.

1 How are the clauses linked to the main part of the sentence?

2 In sentences A–C, what does each relative pronoun refer to?

3 Make the clauses into complete sentences.

6.4 Extending skills writing complex sentences

A Make one sentence for each box on the right, using the method given in red. Include the words in blue. Write the sentences as one paragraph.

Open Diary launched a service which made it possible to create an online diary.
Open Diary made it freely available to anybody.
relative, passive In 1998

Users could comment on other people's diary entries.
Users could decide whether to make their entries public or private.
Users could add other users as their friends.
active, ellipsis Key features

Open Diary laid the foundations of blogging.
Open Diary pioneered key features of social networking.
participle As a result

B Study the notes on the opposite page which a student made about the growth of social networking services.

1 Divide the notes into sections to make suitable paragraphs.

2 Decide which ideas are suitable topic sentences for the paragraphs.

3 Make full sentences from the notes, joining ideas where possible, to make one continuous text.

(A) By 2010, Web 2.0 services which supported online video viewing were causing a drop in P2P traffic.

(B) Three of the many ways in which data transfer has speeded up will be described here.

(C) Ajax also runs mobile web applications which are so useful that they have played an important part in the way in which mobile use has developed.

(D) As well as fully supporting developments such as bulletin boards, server-side scripting made possible services such as Wikipedia.

(E) Having promoted Flash as an essential plug-in, by 2003 its owners saw a huge increase in the proportion of browsers using it.

Table 1: Breaking a complex sentence into constituent parts

	Main S	Main V	Main O/C	Other V + S/O/C	Adv. phrases
A	Web 2.0 services	were causing	a drop in P2P traffic	which supported online video viewing.	By 2010
B					

Background to social networking services (SNS)

- When did SNS begin?
- Friendster – first recognizable SNS – March 2003
- Acquired patents on key SN technology
- MySpace – later 2003 → estab. co., used Frstr. as model
- Facebook launched 2004 → initially limited to US universities ∴ seen as more exclusive
- Rapid growth of SNS = issue
- Frstr. – launch + 3 mths. = 3m users
- By 2005 Frstr. = 60m page views per day
- Facebook – Nov 2008 = 200m unique visitors & 2010 > 500m users (co. data)
- MySpace – Sept 2010 > 120m unique users per month (co. data)
- Care needed in planning architecture
- e.g., Frstr. tech. unable to meet demand in early years ∴ loss of users to other services
- MySpace also performance issues from speed of growth
- Facebook – well-designed architecture ∴ no difficulties in scaling
- Future of SNS
- No. of users continues to grow
- Large nos. of new SNS
- SNS replace search for info → problems for Google
- Privacy and security of user data = issue for future

Reporting findings

You cannot use another writer's words unless you directly quote. Instead, you must restate or **paraphrase**.

There are several useful ways to do this:

use a synonym of a word or phrase	*active* ➔ *dynamic* *data using VoIP protocols* ➔ *VoIP traffic*
change negative to positive and vice versa	*sales rose slowly* ➔ *sales didn't increase quickly*
use a replacement subject	*VoIP traffic was increasing* ➔ *there was an increase in VoIP traffic*
change from active to passive or vice versa	*the cache updated the page* ➔ *the page was updated from the cache*
change the order of information	*in the introduction phase, HTTP usage declined gradually* ➔ *there was a gradual decline in HTTP usage early in the cycle*

When reporting findings from one source, you should use all the methods above, as far as possible.

Example:

Original text	*Streaming more than doubled between 2007 and 2010.*
Report	*The proportion of Internet data using streaming protocols in 2010 was over twice as much as it had been in 2007.*

Important

When paraphrasing, you should aim to make sure that 90% of the words you use are different from the original. It is not enough to change only a few vocabulary items: this will result in plagiarism.

Example:

Original text	*Web 2.0 provided social networking with the tools it needed to develop fully.*
Plagiarism	*Web 2.0 gave social networking the tools it needed to develop fully.*

Finding the main information

Sentences in academic and technical texts are often very long.

Example:
Following the debate at a conference organized by Tim O'Reilly in 2004, a number of Internet theorists agreed that **the term Web 2.0 was useful** *in explaining the changes from a web where users only received data, to one where they exchanged it.*

You often don't have to understand every word, but you must **identify the subject**, **the verb and the object**, if there is one.

For example, in the sentence above, we find:
subject = *the term Web 2.0*
verb = *was*
complement = *useful*

Remember!

You can remove any leading prepositional phrases at this point to help you find the subject, e.g., *Following the debate …*

You can also remove any introductory phrase, e.g. *a number of Internet theorists agreed that …*

You must then find the **main words which modify** the subject, the verb and the object or complement.

In the sentence above we find:

What term? = *Web 2.0*

Why useful? = to explain the change from users only receiving data, to users exchanging data

Ellipsis

Sometimes, if the meaning is clear, words are implied rather than actually given in the text.

Examples:
There are many ways (in which) *data can be transferred.*

The service had a number of key features which allowed users to comment on diary entries from other people, (which allowed users to) *make their entries public or private, and* (which allowed users to) *add other users as their friends.*

7.1 Vocabulary   compound nouns • fixed phrases

A Study the words in box a.

1 Match nouns in column 1 with nouns in column 2 to make compound nouns.

2 Which word in each phrase has the strongest stress?

B Study the phrases in box b.

1 Complete each phrase with one word.

2 Is each phrase followed by:
- a noun (including gerund)?
- subject + verb?
- an infinitive?

3 What is each phrase used for?

C Look at the pictures on the opposite page showing the production process for developing a website. What happens at each stage?

D Read extracts A–F on the right. They are from a leaflet by a web development company.

1 Match each extract with a picture on the opposite page.

2 Complete each sentence with one or more phrases from box b.

E Look at the Gantt chart on the opposite page. What does it show?

F Read the text under the Gantt chart. Match the phrases in box c with the highlighted phrases in the text. Which part of the chart is not mentioned?

G Look at the web pages 1–3 on the opposite page. Complete this small web development company memo using phrases from boxes b and c.

My recommendation is that the design _____ in picture 3 should go into full production. My opinion is _____ personal preference, but also on _____ other points. Firstly, _____ to maximize traffic to the site, we need to _____ the younger age groups. The _____ this type of visitor is important for the success of this site. _____ of this design, the colours are very attractive for younger people. _____ to this, the design emphasizes the simple functionality of the site.

a

1	2
back client design development production project quality system	assurance design end management programming requirements specification tools

b

as shown ...   as well ...   in addition ...
in order ...   in such a way ...
in the case ...   known ...
the end ...   the use ...

A When the prototypes are ready, the client meets the developers _____ to decide which design should go into full production.

B _____ of special software for the initial layout and HTML coding means that a number of prototype sites can be produced very quickly.

C _____ to develop the website, the company works with the client to produce a document _____ a statement of requirements.

D _____ of the development process takes place when the site is uploaded to the company's web servers and goes live.

E These requirements are then analyzed using UML (Unified Modelling Language), _____ in the diagram, and detailed specifications are produced outlining the functionality _____ as the features of the site.

F _____ of more complex sites, the developers will analyze the specifications _____ that they can determine which technologies are most suitable.

c

a number of   a variety of
at the same time
bear in mind   based on   deal with
from the point of view of
the beginning of   the development of

Developing a website

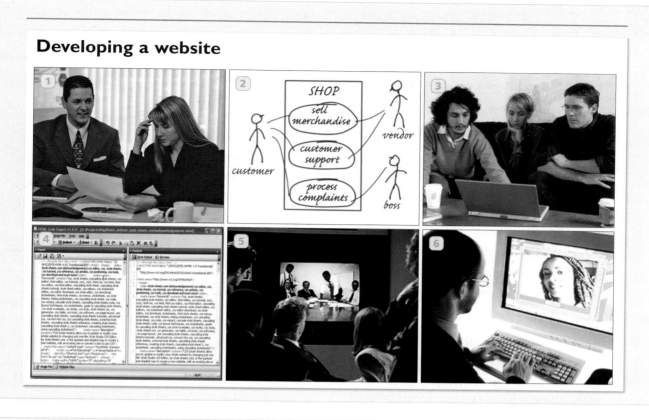

Gantt chart: Developing a new piece of software

	Week 1	Week 2	Week 3	Week 4	Week 5	Week 6	Week 7
Specification document created							
Using UML to decide on design							
Decision on platform and design tools							
Mock-up of front-end design							
Demonstrate models to client for decision							
Production begins							

A Gantt chart is a useful planning tool, especially for project management. The chart makes it easy to handle a situation where different stages overlap. For example, this chart shows some stages of the evolution of a new piece of software. The start of the process involves the creation of a specification document. Then, using the specifications, UML models of the software are made. The developers use various criteria to decide on the best platform and design tools. Simultaneously, mock-ups of the design are created using input from several designers, and a number of models are prepared for the client to choose from.

A You are going to hear the lecture on the right. Write four questions you would like answered.

B 🎧 Listen to Part 1 of the lecture.

1 What is the lecturer going to talk about today? Write *yes*, *no* or *not mentioned*.

- production of code   ____
- design specification   ____
- working prototype   ____
- costs of production   ____
- production methods   ____
- scheduling   ____

2 What is project management?

C 🎧 Listen to Part 2 of the lecture.

1 Make notes in an appropriate form.

2 What is another word for *software*?

3 What activities are involved in defining user requirements for software development? Give some examples.

4 Were your questions in Exercise A answered?

D Match each phrase in the first column of the table on the right with the type of information that can follow.

E 🎧 Listen to Part 3 of the lecture.

1 Makes notes on the information that comes after the phrases in Exercise D.

2 Were your questions in Exercise A answered?

F 🎧 Listen for sentences 1–4 below in Part 4 of the lecture. Which sentence (**a** or **b**) follows in each case? Why? *See Skills bank*

1 Model type one is the waterfall model.
  a In this type of model, each stage directly follows the other.
  b Each stage directly follows the other in this type of model.

2 The iterative model adds functionality in stages to software.
  a Examples of this type of software are things like end-user applications or operating system versions.
  b End-user applications or operating system versions are examples of this type of software.

Faculty: ICT Studies
Computer Software Development (Lecture 1)
Lecture overview
- Software development process
- Technical issues
- Specifying features of software
- Models for software development
- Planning software production and scheduling

Fixed phrase	Followed by ...
1 An important concept (is) ...	a different way to think about the topic
2 What do I mean by ...?	an imaginary example
3 As you can see, ...	a key statement or idea
4 Looking at it another way, ...	a concluding comment giving a result of something
5 In project management terms, ...	a new idea or topic that the lecturer wants to discuss
6 Say ...	a comment about a diagram, or stage
7 The point is ...	an explanation of a word or phrase
8 In this way ...	a general idea put into a specific context

3 The third model is called the prototyping model.
  a In prototyping, the important thing is that clients have an opportunity to see a model before it is fully developed.
  b What's important about prototyping is that clients have an opportunity to see a model before it is fully developed.

4 Lastly, there is the spiral model.
  a In the spiral model, a difference is that it combines elements of both the waterfall and prototyping models.
  b What's different in the spiral model is that it combines elements of both the waterfall and prototyping models.

G This lecturer is not very well organized. What problems are there in the lecture?

7.3 Extending skills

stress within words • fixed phrases • giving sentences a special focus

A 🎧 Listen to some stressed syllables. Identify the word below in each case. Number each word.

Example:

You hear: *1 con* /kɒn/   You write:

concept	__1__	functionality	____	requirements	____
dependent	____	increment	____	resources	____
documentation	____	proprietary	____	specification	____
features	____	prototype	____	spiral	____

B 🎧 Listen to the final part of the lecture from Lesson 2.

1 Complete the notes on the right by adding a symbol in each space.

2 What research task(s) are you asked to do?

C Study the phrases from the lecture in the blue box. For which of the following purposes did the lecturer use each phrase?

- to introduce a new topic
- to emphasize a major point
- to add points
- to finish a list
- to give an example
- to restate

D Rewrite these sentences to give a special focus. Begin with the words in brackets.

1 Henry Gantt came up with an idea to help with scheduling. (*It*)

2 Gantt invented his charts in the early 1900s. (*It*)

3 The choice of development methodology is critical. (*What*)

4 Planning software production is complex because planning decisions are based on a wide variety of different factors. (Two sentences. First = *It*; second = *The reason*)

5 Gantt charts show what processes are happening at any one time. (*The advantage*)

See *Skills bank*

E Choose one section of the lecture. Refer to your notes and give a spoken summary. Use the fixed phrases and ways of giving special focus that you have looked at.

F Work with a partner.

1 Make a Gantt chart for an activity, project or process.

2 Present your chart to another pair. Practise using fixed phrases and ways of giving special focus.

See *Vocabulary bank* and *Skills bank*

Software production planning ____ complex ____

1. some factors ____ outside control of developer ____ clients ____ changes in requirements

2. design ____ development models

Scheduling ____ what processes? When start ____ finish?

Henry Gantt ____ Gantt charts (early 1900s)

Using waterfall model ____ time lost if earlier stages not ready ____ Gantt charts used for scheduling

---

et cetera
In other words, ...
Let's take ...
Let me put it another way.
I almost forgot to mention ...
Not to mention the fact that ...
Plus there's the fact that ...
The fact of the matter is, ...
You've probably heard of ...

A Look at the weblog and the press release headlines on the opposite page.

  1 What does open source mean?

  2 What information will the press releases contain?

  3 What do the graphs show?

B 🎧 Listen to the first extract from a seminar about open source software.

  1 What question will the students discuss?

  2 Why was Netscape's decision surprising?

C 🎧 Listen to Extract 2 of the seminar. Are these sentences true or false?

  1 Open source makes program code available to everyone.

  2 Anyone can contribute to open source programs.

  3 Open source software is the same as free software.

  4 Open source application software is very user friendly.

  5 The potential social benefits of open source software are considerable.

D Study tasks **a–d** below and the phrases in the blue box.

  1 Write a, b, c or d next to each phrase to show its use.

    a introducing

    b asking for clarification

    c agreeing/disagreeing

    d clarifying

  2 🎧 Listen to Extract 2 again to check your answers.

E Work in groups of four to research the main benefits of open source programming. Each person should choose a different aspect.

- Student A: read about *security* issues on page 102.
- Student B: read about *costs* on page 105.
- Student C: read about *flexibility* on page 105.
- Student D: read about *social issues* on page 106.

After reading the notes, report back orally to your group. Use fixed phrases to ask for and give clarification.

F Work in groups. Choose some of the items shown in the photographs.

  1 Have a practice seminar in which you decide which of the items would benefit from using open source software.

  2 Report to the class on your discussion, giving reasons for your decisions.

I'd like to make two points. First, …	_____
Can you expand on that?	_____
The point is …	_____
What's your second point?	_____
My second point is that …	_____
Yes, but …	_____
I don't agree with that because …	_____
Sorry, but who are we talking about, exactly?	_____
We need to be clear here.	_____
I'd just like to say that …	_____
In what way?	_____
What I'm trying to say is, …	_____
Can you give me an example?	_____
Look at it this way.	_____
Absolutely.	_____

www.VenturesInWonderlandBlog.com

Press Release:
Netscape's decision to go open source revisited

Press Release:
Does open source 'change the game' for software?

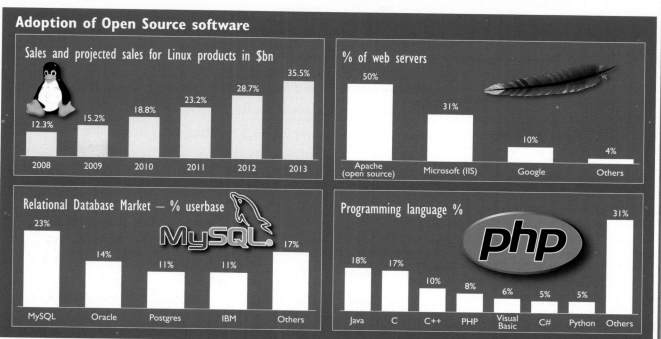

Adoption of Open Source software

Sales and projected sales for Linux products in $bn

2008	2009	2010	2011	2012	2013
12.3%	15.2%	18.8%	23.2%	28.7%	35.5%

% of web servers

Apache (open source)	Microsoft (IIS)	Google	Others
50%	31%	10%	4%

Relational Database Market — % userbase

MySQL	Oracle	Postgres	IBM	Others
23%	14%	11%	11%	17%

Programming language %

Java	C	C++	PHP	Visual Basic	C#	Python	Others
18%	17%	10%	8%	6%	5%	5%	31%

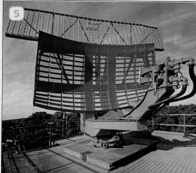

1 cash machine
2 desktop computer
3 lottery ball picking machine
4 mobile phone
5 airfield radar system

Recognizing fixed phrases from ICT (1)

There are many fixed phrases in the field of ICT.

Examples:

Phrase	Meaning in the discipline
back end	combination of database and programming language providing data for dynamic web pages
operating system	software on which the application programs run
development tools	software which is used to write other software programs
open source	software where the source code is freely available

Keep a list of fixed phrases used in ICT and remind yourself regularly of the meaning.

Recognizing fixed phrases from academic English (1)

There are also a large number of fixed phrases which are commonly used in academic and technical English in general.

Examples:

Phrase	What comes next?
As we have seen …	a reminder of previous information
An important concept is …	one of the basic points underlying the topic
As you can see, …	a reference to an illustration OR a logical conclusion from previous information
As shown in …	a reference to a diagram or table
… in such a way that …	a result of something
In addition to (X, Y)	X = reminder of last point, Y = new point
As well as (X, Y)	
In the case of …	a reference to a particular topic or, more often, sub topic
At the same time, …	an action or idea which must be considered alongside another action or idea
… based on …	a piece of research, a theory, an idea
Bear in mind (that) …	key information which helps to explain (or limit in some way) previous information
The point is …	the basic information underlying an explanation
in order to (do X, Y)	X = objective, Y = necessary actions/conditions
In project management terms, …	the importance in relation to project management, of something previously mentioned
In other words, …	the same information put in a different way
Looking at it another way, …	
In this way …	a result from previous information
Say …	an example
What do I mean by (X)?	an explanation of X

Make sure you know what kind of information comes next.

'Given' and 'new' information in sentences

In English, we can put important information at the beginning or at the end of a sentence. There are two types of important information.

1 Information which the listener or reader already knows, from general knowledge or from previous information in the text. This can be called 'given' information. It normally goes at the beginning of the sentence.

2 Information which is new in this text. This can be called 'new' information. It normally goes at the end of a sentence.

Example:

In Lesson 2, the lecturer is talking about production methods, so production methods in general = given information.

Given	New
Model type 1	*is the waterfall model.*
In this type of model,	*each stage directly follows the other.*

Giving sentences a special focus

We sometimes change the normal word order to emphasize a particular point, e.g., a person, an object, a time.

Examples:

Normal sentence	*Henry Gantt invented the Gantt chart in the 1900s.*
Focusing on person	*It was Henry Gantt who invented …*
Focusing on object	*It was the Gantt chart which Henry Gantt invented …*
Focusing on time	*It was in the early 1900s that Gantt …*

Introducing new information

We can use special structures to introduce a new topic.

Examples:
Software production methods are my subject today.
  → **What I am going to talk about today is** *software production methods.*

Agreeing a statement of requirements with the client is very important.
  → **What is very important is** *agreeing a statement of requirements with the client.*

Client changes can cause problems to arise.
  → **The reason why problems can arise is** *client changes.*

Poor planning leads to project failure.
  → **The result of poor planning is** *project failure.*

Clarifying points

When we are speaking, we often have to clarify points. There are many expressions which we can use.

Examples:
Let me put it another way …   *What I'm trying to say is …*
Look at it this way …   *The point/thing is …*

8.1 Vocabulary
synonyms • nouns from verbs • paraphrasing

A Look at the pictures opposite.

   1 Match pictures A–G with the appropriate labels 1–7.

   2 What functions do the items in pictures A–F perform in the FuTek system in diagram G?

B Discuss the following questions.

   1 What is meant by *efficiency* in computer systems?

   2 What can be used to measure the *efficiency* of the items in box a?

C Look up each noun in box b in a dictionary.

   1 Is it countable, uncountable or both?

   2 What is its meaning in ICT?

   3 What is a good synonym?

   4 What useful grammatical information can you find?

D Study the two lists of verbs in box c.

   1 Match the verbs with similar meanings.

   2 Make nouns from the verbs if possible.

E Look at the Hadford University handout.

   1 How does the writer restate each section heading in the paragraph?

   2 Find synonyms for the blue words and phrases. Use a dictionary if necessary.

   3 Rewrite each sentence to make paraphrases of the texts. Use:

- synonyms you have found yourself
- synonyms from Exercise C
- the nouns you made in Exercise D
- passives where possible
- any other words that are necessary

   Example:
Centralizing data-processing operations can play a role in developing efficient systems.

   ➔ *The centralization of data-processing operations can contribute to greater efficiency in a computer system.*

F Study the pictures of the computer system on the opposite page again.

   1 What changes might improve the performance of the system?

   2 What possible problems might result from these changes?

---

a

interface	network	processors
software	storage	support

b

cost	data centre	function
migration	outage	processor
	task	utilization

c

	1	2
	cluster	interrupt
	consume	guarantee
	convert	contribute (to)
	disrupt	reduce
	distribute	include
	drive down	group
	ensure	transform
	incorporate	balance, share
	mask	assess
	measure	use
	play a role in	hide

HADFORD *University*

Efficiency in systems development

A Data centre migration
Moving processing and storage operations to a centralized location can play a role in developing efficient systems. For example, by using multiple servers clustered together on one site, and software to distribute the processing load across them, higher utilization levels can be obtained. This drives down the cost of hardware, so systems using data centres can deliver services more cheaply.

B Capacity utilization
We can measure how well a system is using its resources (i.e., processor, memory) like this: actual usage divided by maximum potential usage times 100. All designers try to lower the cost of processing in a system. One way to do this is to use efficient software to minimize the amount of spare capacity.

Parts of a system

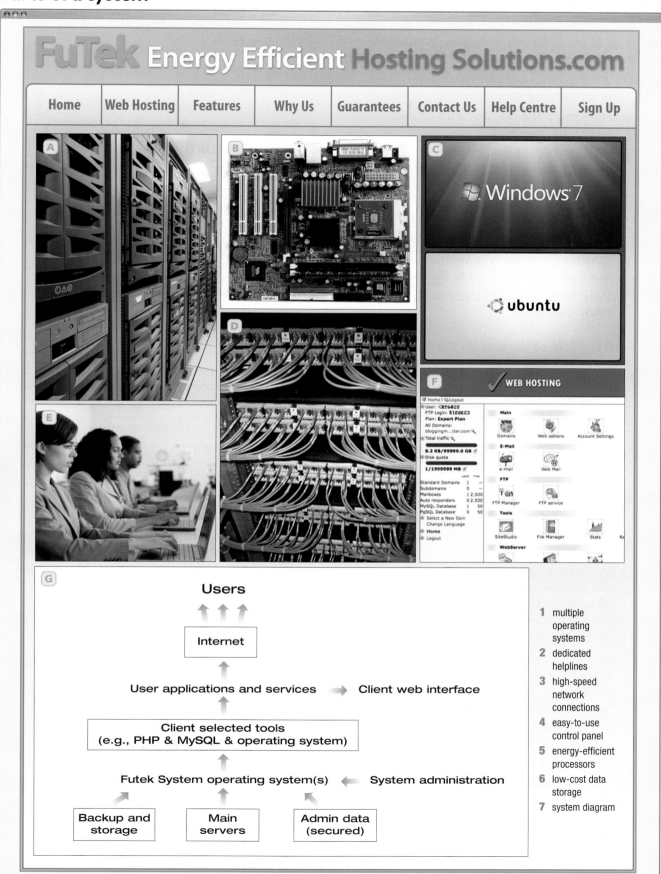

FuTek Energy Efficient Hosting Solutions.com

| Home | Web Hosting | Features | Why Us | Guarantees | Contact Us | Help Centre | Sign Up |

Users

Internet

User applications and services → Client web interface

Client selected tools
(e.g., PHP & MySQL & operating system)

Futek System operating system(s) ← System administration

Backup and storage | Main servers | Admin data (secured)

1 multiple operating systems
2 dedicated helplines
3 high-speed network connections
4 easy-to-use control panel
5 energy-efficient processors
6 low-cost data storage
7 system diagram

A Look at the different examples of systems in the blue box.

1 What type of system is each one (e.g., e-mail = communication system)?

2 How could the performance of each system be improved?

3 What changes could be made to each system to bring about these improvements?

B Look at the four essay types on the right.

1 What should the writer do in each type?

2 Match each essay type with one of the questions below the slide (A–D).

3 What topics should be covered in each essay question?

C Read the title of the text on the opposite page and the first sentence of each paragraph.

1 What will the text be about?

2 Choose one of the essay questions in Exercise B. Write four research questions which will help you to find information for your essay.

D Read the text.

1 Using your own words, make notes from the text on information for your essay question.

2 Work with another person who has chosen the same essay question as you. Compare your notes.

E Study the highlighted sentences in the text.

1 Underline all the subjects and their verbs.

2 Which is the main subject and verb for each sentence?

F Study the table on the right.

1 Match each word or phrase with its meaning.

2 Underline the words or phrases in the text which the writer uses to give the definitions.

See Vocabulary bank

---

air traffic control   e-mail
nuclear power plant   patient record
search engine   social networking

HADFORD *University*

There are four main essay types in ICT:

- descriptive
- analytical
- comparison/evaluation
- argument

A What are the advantages and disadvantages of virtualization for large commercial organizations?

B 'Virtualization answers all of the questions which system designers have to ask about hardware.' To what extent do you agree with this statement?

C Explain why reducing system energy consumption is essential to the success of virtualization.

D What questions do designers need to ask when considering the efficiency of their systems? Describe how two companies have found different answers to some of these questions.

Word/phrase	Meaning
1 'out-of-the box'	where physical components can be added or removed without shutting down the system
2 data integrity	ensuring that devices operate efficiently whether they are idle, operating at lower usage levels, or at full capacity
3 energy proportionality	circuits on the computer's motherboard providing the voltages required by the microchips
4 'hot swapping'	systems supplying power with built in storage capacity so that during a power outage servers can keep running
5 uninterruptible power supplies (UPS)	equipment provided by the manufacturer without modification
6 voltage regulator circuitry	ensuring that data is not corrupted

'Hiding the hardware':

Using virtual machines to improve system efficiency

Good system design has always tried to balance performance and cost. For designers of generalized commercial systems, this has meant a careful analysis of the specifications of component parts, to ensure that they can provide the necessary functionality and reliability at the least possible cost. Where systems are a key element of commercial organizations, the level of system efficiency can mean the difference between success and failure for a company.

Here is a list of questions which have to be considered by systems designers:

- What can be done to minimize system hardware costs?
- What is the best balance between the level of specification of hardware components in a system, and their cost?
- What are the implications of these changes on the overall operation of the system?
- How easily will the system architecture 'scale up': that is, increase proportionally, if it needs to be expanded?
- How can systems be designed to minimize their effects on the environment?

Some answers to the above questions have been provided by *virtualization*. A key concept of virtualization is *clustering*, which means locating the hardware elements of the system together in a data centre or server farm. This makes it easier to provide an optimal environment for the hardware to work in. System maintenance is also simplified by clustering, as it makes components easily accessible for repair or replacement. Another concept is *masking*, which involves making the physical components of the system appear as one virtual device to system administrators. This makes it easier for them to manage the system. Virtualization can be used for servers, storage and networking. A key benefit of virtualization is that physical components can be added or removed without shutting down the system (this is known as '*hot swapping*'). This provides great flexibility for system designers as it means that processing, networking or storage capacity can be scaled up or down very quickly in response to changes in the business environment.

In addition to flexibility in system size, virtualization allows flexibility in terms of the specification of system components which can be used, although there are limitations. The system developer's choice of components is limited by the level of reliability required by the system. For example, 'out-of-the-box' servers, which are those purchased from manufacturers without modification, are typically both expensive and high specification. They are ideal for e-commerce companies such as Amazon which require very high levels of reliability and data integrity (ensuring that data is not corrupted). For others, such as Google, reliability is less important than cost because the amount of revenue which they obtain from each search is so small. For this reason, they have used enormous numbers of low-cost, low-specification PCs. These are less reliable, but using virtualization means that the failure of a component, such as a motherboard, will not disrupt the service overall. Any loss of data will only affect transactions taking place at the time. For search engine systems such as Google, this may simply mean users not getting the optimum search results. For other types of systems, the effects may be more damaging.

Large amounts of power are required to cool data centres, which has led to a widespread recognition of the impact of virtualization on global warming. The size of this impact can be seen in a 2006 US EPA (Environmental Protection Agency) report. This stated that data centres accounted for 1.5 % of all US electricity consumption, and that the technology they used had to be improved if their rate of growth was to be sustained. For example, most data centres use *chillers*, which are elaborate water-based cooling systems, to maintain an appropriate temperature for the hardware. However, some companies, such as Google, have begun an initiative to avoid the use of chillers and to reduce power consumption by relying on innovative data centre design. One approach is to use only DC current in the centres, avoiding conversion losses from standard AC current. By using higher specification voltage regulator circuitry – circuits on the computer's motherboard providing the voltages required by the microchips – more power savings can be made. In fact, all server components are designed to have a property called *energy proportionality*, which ensures that they operate efficiently whether they are idle (not doing any active work), operating at lower usage levels, or at full capacity. By giving each server its own battery, Google avoids using *uninterruptible power supplies* (UPS), a term used for giant batteries which ensure that servers keep running if there is a power outage. These consume large amounts of energy. While Google has long been recognized as a leader in data centre energy efficiency, Yahoo is catching up. By 2014, Yahoo plans to have data centres which will be more energy efficient than those currently used by Google, according to a Yahoo corporate blog on 30th June 2009.

A Find the words in the blue box in the text in Lesson 8.2.

1 What part of speech is each word?

2 Think of another word which could be used in place of the word in the text. Use your dictionary if necessary.

> component   reliability   scale up
> key   environment
> transactions   widespread
> impact   chillers   appropriate
> initiative   motherboard

B Study sentences A–D which relate to the text in Lesson 8.2.

1 Identify the dependent clause.

2 Copy the table under the sentences and write the parts of each dependent clause in the table.

3 Rewrite the sentence using an active construction.

Example:
Here is a list of questions which systems designers have to consider.

C Read the essay plans and extracts on the opposite page.

1 Match each plan with an essay title in Lesson 8.2.

2 Which essay is each extract from?

3 Which part of the plan is each extract from?

D Work with a partner.

1 Write another paragraph for one of the plans.

2 Exchange paragraphs with another pair. Can they identify where it comes from?

A | Here is a list of questions which have to be considered by systems designers.

B | Google has designed innovative systems in which power consumption is reduced.

C | Energy costs are high when data centres are cooled by chillers.

D | Amazon uses thousands of servers which are provided by a number of different manufacturers.

Subject	Verb	By whom/what
(questions) which	have to be considered	systems designers

A Make complete sentences from these notes. Add words as necessary.

A   suggested – virtualization – answer – all key questions – systems designers – ask – systems hardware

B   virtualization – provide answer – many – not all – questions– ask – systems designers

C   ease – maintenance – ability – system – respond – change – among – questions – answered – virtualization

D   addressing question – key task – determine – questions virtualization answers – whether questions – doesn't answer

E   virtualization – process – physical hardware components – clustered – combined – create – virtual machine

F   questions – virtualization not answer – concern specification – components – reliability – issues relating – energy consumption

B The sentences in Exercise A are topic sentences for paragraphs in essay B in Lesson 8.2. Put them in the best order for the essay. What is the main topic for each paragraph?

C Look at the essay question on the right.

1 What kind of essay is this?

2 Do some research and make a plan.

3 Write the essay.

See *Skills bank*

Essay question

> Yahoo aims to overtake Google in energy efficiency in its data centres. Describe the steps that Yahoo will need to take in order to make this happen.

Essay plans

A

1 Introduction: importance of system efficiency; aims of essay.

2 Define system efficiency.

3 Some questions to be considered: hardware cost v. need for reliability, minimizing effect on environment.

4 Examples: Google using low-spec. PCs to minimize hardware cost, Amazon high-spec. to ensure data integrity. Economic implications in terms of transactions.

5 Conclusion: different company requirements will mean different answers to some of these questions.

B

1 Introduction: importance of energy saving; give essay aims.

2 Definition of virtualization.

3 Widespread recognition of the impact of virtualization on global warming: levels of energy use, clustering of hardware in data centres, use of chillers for cooling.

4 Innovative techniques to improve efficiency: use of batteries to replace UPS, higher-spec. components for energy saving, use of DC power as standard.

5 Increasing importance of global warming as political issue. Need for energy savings where possible.

6 Conclusion: without energy saving, likely limitations on growth of virtualization.

Essay extracts

It is important to acknowledge that there has been widespread recognition of the impact of virtualization on global warming. As a 2006 US EPA report pointed out, at the time, data centres were using 1.5% of the electricity produced in the United States. The report also recommended that the technology used by the data centres needed to be improved if their growth was to continue at the same pace. However, because virtualization requires large amounts of hardware to be clustered together, it would appear that some means of cooling is necessary. Currently, a high proportion of data centres use chillers – elaborate water-based cooling systems – to maintain an appropriate temperature for the hardware. The evidence suggests that these are not always required, as the example of Google has shown.

In considering these questions, it is worth looking at the way in which Google has minimized hardware costs by using low-cost PCs rather than 'out-of-the-box' servers. Because of the low revenue per search received by Google, it is essential that the cost of each transaction is kept as low as possible. The effect of a loss of data from component failure is relatively limited. At worst, it may mean that the user has to re-run a search.

Understanding new words: using definitions

You will often find new words in academic texts. Sometimes you will not be able to understand the text unless you look the word up in a dictionary, but often a technical term will be defined or explained immediately or later in the text.

Look for these indicators:

is or *are*	*'Virtualization' is basically about …*
brackets	*… its data centre (server farms).*
or	*… most data centres use chillers, or water-based cooling systems, to …*
which	*… 'out-of-the-box' servers, which are those purchased from manufacturers without modification …*
a comma or a dash (–) immediately after the word or phrase	*… uninterruptible power supplies (UPS) – giant batteries which …*
phrases such as *that is, in other words*	*… component load rates: that is, the work performed by each system component. In other words, how often the components …*

Remember!

When you write assignments, you may want to define words yourself. Learn to use the methods above to give variety to your written work.

Understanding direction verbs in essay titles

Special verbs called **direction verbs** are used in essay titles. Each direction verb indicates a type of essay. You must understand the meaning of these words so you can choose the correct writing plan.

Kind of essay	Direction verbs
Descriptive	*State … Say … Outline … Describe … Summarize … What is/are …?*
Analytical	*Analyze … Explain … Comment on … Examine … Give reasons for … Why …? How …?*
Comparison/ Evaluation	*Compare (and contrast) … Distinguish between … Evaluate … What are the advantages and/or disadvantages of …?*
Argument	*Discuss … Consider … (Critically) evaluate … To what extent …? How far …?*

Choosing the correct writing plan

When you are given a written assignment, you must decide on the best writing plan before you begin to write the outline. Use key words in the essay title to help you choose – see *Vocabulary bank*.

Type of writing assignment – content	Possible structure
Descriptive writing List **the most important points** of something: e.g., a list of key events in chronological order; history of a computer system; a description of a process, detailing each step and what the outcome of each step might be. Summarize points in a logical order. **Example**: *What are the key features of virtualization?* *Describe the impact of innovative system design on reducing data centre power consumption.*	• **introduction** • **description of process/system** • **point/step 1/outcome** • **point/step 2/outcome** • **point/step 3/outcome** • **conclusion**
Analytical writing List **the important points** which **in your opinion** explain the situation. Justify your opinion in each case. Look behind the facts at the **how** and **why**, not just **what/who/when**. Look for and question accepted ideas and assumptions. **Example**: *Explain the appeal of virtualization to systems designers.*	• **introduction** • **definitions** • **most important point:** example/evidence/reason 1, example/evidence/reason 2, etc. • **next point:** example/evidence/reason 3, example/evidence/reason 4, etc. • **conclusion**
Comparison/evaluation (may incorporate case studies) Decide on and define the **aspects** to compare two subjects. You may use these aspects as the basis for paragraphing. Evaluate which aspect(s) is/are better or preferable and give reasons/criteria for your judgement. **Example:** *Compare the use of high- and low-spec components when designing a system.* *Compare how Amazon and Google may have approached the design of their systems to ensure user satisfaction.*	• **introduction** • **state and define aspects** *Either*: • **aspect 1:** subject A v. B • **aspect 2:** subject A v. B *Or*: • **subject A:** aspect 1, 2, etc. • **subject B:** aspect 1, 2, etc. • **conclusion/evaluation**
Argument writing (may incorporate case studies) Analyze and/or evaluate, then give your opinion in a statement at the beginning or the end. Show awareness of difficulties and disagreements by mentioning counter-arguments. Support your opinion with evidence. **Example:** *'Virtualization can provide significant flexibility in systems design'. Discuss this with reference to two companies.*	• **introduction: statement of issue** • **statement giving opinion** • **define terms** • **point 1:** explain + evidence • **point 2:** explain + evidence, etc. • **conclusion** implications, etc. *Alternatively*: • **introduction: statement of issue** • **define terms** • **for:** point 1, 2, etc. • **against:** point 1, 2, etc. • **conclusion: statement of opinion**

A Match the words to make fixed phrases.

1	development ☐	a	assurance
2	hardware ☐	b	development
3	project ☐	c	device
4	quality ☐	d	display
5	system ☐	e	interface
6	user ☐	f	management
7	visual ☐	g	method
8	input ☐	h	specifications

1	2
a	... start with
	... people think
to	on ... other hand
the	to ... extent
	on ... one hand
some	... real question is
many	on ... grounds that
	... would be great, except
this	in ... case like this
that	in ... sort of situation

B Study the words and phrases in the blue box.

1 Complete each phrase in column 2 with a word from column 1.

2 Which phrase(s) can you use to:
  - agree only partly with a point?
  - begin talking about several points?
  - talk about a particular example?
  - introduce the first of two ideas?
  - introduce the second of two ideas?
  - focus on the most important point?
  - give a reason for a point?
  - talk about certain circumstances?
  - mention a problem with someone's idea?

C On the opposite page are some people who have an interest in a new product being developed.

1 Match each person with the correct job title.

2 What aspects of human–computer interaction (HCI) is each person interested in? Why?

3 Match each person with the correct quote (A–F).

4 Replace the words in italics with a phrase from Exercise B.

D Read the extract from the Hadford University handout about human–computer interaction.

1 Match the blue words in this extract with the definitions A–L on the opposite page.

2 Use your dictionary to check words you do not know.

E Complete the table on the right.

HADFORD *University*

HCI draws on psychology and computer science in order to provide user-friendly interfaces for computers. For example:

- Cognitive psychology provides models of perceptual, motor and cognitive systems by which humans interact with the world.
- An engineering approach to the senses sees visual, aural and haptic data as channels for input or output.
- Designers of input devices need to consider their responsiveness, usability and ergonomics.
- Heuristic evaluation can identify problems with the design of a user interface.
- Familiar metaphors in interface design help users create mental models of system objects quickly.
- User input which completes one or more tasks in an action sequence, to achieve a specific goal within the domain they are working in.

Base form	Other related forms	
constrain	constraint	constrained
evaluation		
intuition		
manipulate		
measure		
navigate		
observe		
response		
sequence		
use		

- company executive
- hardwear designer
- system tester
- interface designer
- psychologist
- project manager

A '*Usually* prototype consoles are not very intuitive, but I was able to find most of the functions on this one really quickly.'

B 'There are several things I have to consider. *Firstly*, what resources do I have to deliver this product?'

C 'We have increased the amount of memory, *but* the size of the processor is the same.'

D '*They say* that we just have to have better technology than the competition to increase profits. I *don't agree completely*, but it is clear that improved system performance is a major factor in selling lots of units.'

E 'We have lots of new functions on the console, but *the important thing is* whether users can access them easily.'

F 'I did some tests with users to evaluate various metaphors the designers want to use in the interface *because* these could help improve intuitiveness.'

---

www.hadfield.ac.uk/biz/def

Definitions

A a number of actions which follow each other, usually in order to attain a specific goal

B a specific area within which a goal is to be achieved

C an objective which an individual or system is trying to achieve

D data input into a computer system by a user

E data which is generated by or related to touch

F design of equipment to reduce user fatigue, discomfort and injury

G designing the interactions between end users and computer systems

H this carries information from the individual's environment to the cognitive and motor systems

I this is the part of the human system which is responsible for controlling movement

J this system processes information to perform work such as knowing, understanding, deciding and problem solving

K where a software object represents a real-world object, or object used in other software (e.g., scissors icon to represent cutting)

L a method for finding the usability problems in a user interface design

A Study the slide on the right. What questions do you think the lecturer will answer?

B Listen to Part 1 of the lecture.

1 Complete the *Notes* section below.

2 What is the lecturer's story about? Why is it not given in the notes?

3 Complete the *Summary* section.

4 Answer the *Review* questions.

C Create a blank Cornell diagram. Listen to Part 2 of the lecture.

1 Complete the *Notes* section.

2 Write some *Review* questions.

3 Complete the *Summary* section.

4 Were your questions in Exercise A answered?

D Study the phrases in column 1 of the blue box. Listen to some sentences from the lecture. Which type of information in column 2 follows each phrase?

 **HADFORD** *University*

Human-computer interaction

- Human sciences – psychology, social disciplines, organizational knowledge
- Computer sciences – hardware, software, devices
- Computer-based usability evaluation methods

1	2
1 Research has shown that …	a developing trend
2 It could be argued that …	information about a point the speaker will make later
3 As we shall see …	
4 From the point of view of …	an aspect of a topic the speaker wants to focus on
5 Increasingly, we find that …	a statement the speaker agrees with
6 It's true to say that …	a conclusion
7 In terms of …	
8 So it should be clear that …	an idea the speaker may not agree with

	Review	Notes
	2 components of HCI are?	HCI = 2: human sci. (HS) and computer sci. (CS)
	Importance of HCI means …?	HCI is _____ ⟶ various _____
		⟶ system designers draw on HS + _____
	HS	**HS**
	1 Main purpose of HS …?	1 _____ how users interact - world and comp:
	System designers draw on …?	• cog. psych., soc. disciplines, org. knowl.
	Aims of HS?	• aim to help system designers
	(5 specific aims)	(1) decide on approach to _____ design
		(2) model human input and output _____ (e.g., visual aural, _____)
		(3) help evaluate _____ (e.g., folder)
		(4) provide _____ tools - quality
		(5) identify likely points of _____
	2 Main model?	2 Main model = Model Human Processor (MHP) modelling human information _____ (perceptual, motor, cognitive).
	3 Design & quality techniques (advantages: why used? by whom?)	3 Improves usability, user experience:
		• empirical ⟶ _____ are based on data
		• particularly useful for _____ designers
	Summary	

9.3 Extending skills

recognizing digressions • understanding spoken source references

A Study the words and phrases in box a.

1 Mark the stressed syllables.

2 🎧 Listen and check your answers.

3 Which word or phrase in each group has a different stress pattern?

a

1 visual, input, design, haptic, output

2 mental model, user input, visual display, input device, action sequence

3 actually, generally, usually, ideally, crucially

B Study the phrases in box b.

1 Do you think the phrases show a digression (start or end) or a relevant point? Write **D** or **R**.

2 Look at the **D** phrases. Do they start or end the digression?

C 🎧 Listen to the final part of the lecture from Lesson 9.2.

1 Take notes using the Cornell system. Leave spaces if you miss information.

2 What topic does the lecturer mention that is different from the main subject?

3 Why does the lecturer mention this topic?

4 What is the research task?

5 Compare your notes in pairs. Fill in any blank spaces.

6 Complete the *Review* and *Summary* sections.

b

Now, where was I?

It's the first of these points that I'm going to focus on now …

By the way, …

So to get back to the main part …

I have a little story to tell you …

If we move on now to …

You don't need to take notes on this …

The point of that story is …

If we turn now to …

When we look at tools from the computer sciences, we'll find …

D 🎧 What information does the lecturer provide about sources? Listen to the extracts and complete the table below.

	Extract 1	Extract 2	Extract 3	Extract 4
Name of writer				
Title and date of source				
Location				
Type of reference				
Relevant to …?				
Introducing phrase				

E Use your notes to write 75–100 words about methods of evaluating interface usability, drawing on the human sciences.

F Work in groups. Study the four methods of usability testing linked to the human sciences in box c. Choose one type you would like to find out more about and then discuss these questions.

1 What kind of information will you need to find?

2 What ideas do you have already?

3 Where can you go to find more information?

c

task, user and environment analysis

focus group

cognitive walkthrough

thinking aloud

A Look at the words in the blue box. Identify their stress patterns.

acceleration   approach   constraint

evaluation   innovation   interaction

interface   limitation   metaphor

B Work in pairs.

Student A: Think of good ways to take part in a seminar.

Student B: Think of bad ways to take part in a seminar.

C You are going to hear some students in a seminar. They have been asked to discuss the question: 'What can computer-based methods contribute to usability testing?'

1 🎧 Listen to the four seminar extracts. Decide whether each contribution is good or poor.

2 Give reasons for your opinion.

3 Think of some more information to add to the good contributions.

D Work in groups of three or four.

1 Discuss your information for the topics in Lesson 9.3, Exercise F. Agree on the best definition.

2 Discuss how best to present this information.

3 Present a definition and description of your topic to the whole class.

E Study Figure 1 and Figure 2.

1 What do the pictures in Figure 1 show?

2 Study the information in Figure 2 on the opposite page. In pairs or groups, discuss the following:

a What does the information show about Interactivity Unlimited?

b What other evaluation methods could Interactivity Unlimited have used?

c Look at the user comments. What problems with the web interface design could have caused these?

d Which interfaces do you think E-Tail should concentrate on improving? Tell the class about your decision, saying what it is based on.

Figure 1

Interactivity Unlimited (IU) is a consultancy which helps clients get the best possible results from their websites and digital system interfaces. Our usability consultants employ a wide range of tools to find out what users want from their interactions, and to ensure that the interfaces can provide these in a user-friendly way. We also consider the ergonomics of devices.

E-Tail Ltd provides four different versions of its website for users to access: computer Internet browser, conventional mobile, smart phone and TV. IU recently conducted an evaluation of the usability of the E-Tail site. Our report highlights some of the important issues to consider in website design, particularly in relation to mobile devices. Our research used a combination of computer-based and human sciences-based methodologies. To begin with, a focus group of volunteers used the different interfaces on a regular basis. This was followed by an heuristic evaluation, using sets of five evaluators working independently.

These are our suggestions for improving the usability of the smart phone site:

- Use auto-complete to speed up filling in forms.
- Limit the size of the site, so that it fits on the screen more easily.
- Keep the number of clicks needed to get to information to a minimum.
- Ensure that clickable items are separated by enough white space so the user does not click on the wrong link.

> "It took ages before the graphics appeared when I loaded a new page" **smart phone user**

> "It was really text heavy and I had to read everything twice" **mobile phone user**

> "I wasn't sure what to do to get onto the next page" **TV user**

> "It took me a long time to find what I was looking for" **PC user**

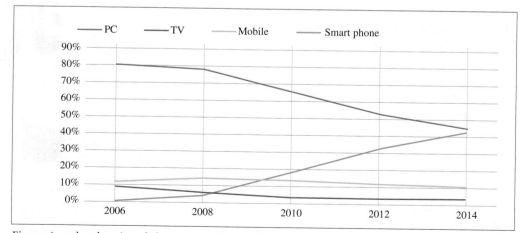

Figure: Actual and projected changes in website traffic by device

Figure 2: *HCI report on E-Tail Ltd website by Interactivity Unlimited*

Recognizing fixed phrases from HCI

Make sure you understand these phrases from HCI.

action sequence

aural data

cognitive psychology

cognitive systems

cognitive walkthrough

eye tracking

focus group

haptic data

heuristic evaluation

input device

interface design

motor system

output device

perceptual system

system logging

task analysis

thinking aloud

usability testing

user analysis

user input

visual data

Recognizing fixed phrases from academic English (2)

Make sure you understand these fixed phrases from general spoken academic English.

As we shall see, …

But the real question is …

From the point of view of …

In a case like this, …

In terms of …

In the sense that …

In this sort of situation, …

That's the reason why …

Increasingly we find that …

It could be argued that …

It's true to say that …

Many people think that …

On the grounds that …

On the one hand, …

On the other hand, …

Research has shown that …

So it should be clear that …

That would be great, except …

To some extent …

To start with, …

Using the Cornell note-taking system

There are many ways to take notes from a lecture. One method was developed by Walter Pauk at Cornell University, USA.

The system involves **Five Rs**.

record	Take notes during the lecture.
reduce	After the lecture turn the notes into one- or two-word questions or 'cues' which will help you remember the key information.
recite	Say the questions and answers aloud.
reflect	Decide on the best way to summarize the key information in the lecture.
review	Look again at the key words and the summary (and do this regularly).

Recognizing digressions

Lecturers sometimes move away from the main point in a lecture to tell a story or an anecdote. This is called a **digression**. You must be able to recognize the start and end of digressions in a lecture.

Sometimes a digression is directly relevant to the content of the lecture, sometimes it has some relevance and sometimes, with a poor lecturer, it may be completely irrelevant. Sometimes the lecturer points out the relevance.

Don't worry if you get lost in a digression. Just leave a space in your notes and ask people afterwards.

Recognizing the start	That reminds me …
	I remember once …
	By the way, …
Recognizing the end	Anyway, where was I?
	Back to the point.
	So, as I was saying …

Understanding the relevance	Of course, the point of that story is …
	I'm sure you can all see that the story shows …
	Why did I tell that story? Well, …

Asking about digressions	What was the point of the story about the interface for a manufacturing system?
	Why did the lecturer start talking about note-taking?
	I didn't get the bit about …

Referring to other people's ideas

We often need to talk about the ideas of other people in a lecture or a tutorial. We normally give the name of the writer and the name of the source. We usually introduce the reference with a phrase; we may quote directly, or we may paraphrase an idea.

Name and introducing phrase	As Dix points out …
	To quote Dix …
Where	in human-computer interaction …
What	we can think of feedback as …

10 E-COMMERCE AND E-GOVERNMENT

'neutral' and 'marked' words • expressing confidence/tentativeness

A Study the words in box a.

1 Use your dictionary to find out the meanings.

2 What part of speech is each word?

B Read the Hadford University handout.

1 Use your dictionary or another source to check the meanings of the highlighted phrases.

2 Which are the stressed syllables in each phrase? Which two phrases have the same stress pattern?

C Look at the pictures on the opposite page.

1 What does each picture show?

2 For each picture, discuss how e-commerce has changed the ways in which transactions or procedures can now be conducted. Use the highlighted phrases from Exercise B and words from Exercise A.

D Study the words in box b.

> **b** brilliant   collapse   enormous
> huge   insignificant   massive   minimal
> outstanding   plummet   plunge
> rocket   significant   slump
> soar   superb   tremendous

1 Check the meanings, parts of speech and stress patterns.

2 Put the words into the correct box in the table below, as in the example.

Neutral	Marked
rise, increase	rocket, soar
fall, decrease	
big, large	
good	
small	

E Read the script from a news programme on e-commerce.

1 Use a marked word in place of each of the blue (neutral) words.

2 Look at the red phrases. How strong are they?

> **a** adopt   bandwidth   barrier   billing
> encrypt   infrastructure   legislation
> penetration   procurement   regulatory
> security   transaction   trust

HADFORD *University*

E-commerce and e-government

E-commerce or electronic commerce describes commercial transactions which take place using electronic communication methods such as the Internet. It takes many different forms, such as the sale of goods and services between businesses (B2B), or from businesses to consumers (B2C). For many retail companies, 'bricks and mortar' shops are being replaced by virtual storefronts on the Internet, challenging the status quo. Consumers can also sell to other consumers (C2C) using online auction sites such as eBay. These sites display the goods for sale, offer dispute resolution services in the event of disagreement and also facilitate payment collection. Governments use e-tendering for procurement (B2G) and increasingly they are using the same technologies for non-commercial transactions, such as providing government information and submitting government forms.

It's clear that the failure of Boo.com in the late 1990s was largely due to its technology. It's generally accepted that their web pages were large and could not be easily downloaded by users with small amounts of bandwidth. It's unlikely that more than a small number of potential customers were able to access the site. As a result, the company's share price fell dramatically, losing a large amount of investors' money ($130 million).

It's fair to say that lastminute.com owed much of its survival to its good website design. Their pages were easily navigable and were small enough to download quickly, providing a good user experience, which undoubtedly contributed to the rising number of sales. The different products sold by the two companies may also have been a factor. While online sales of travel products grew from the beginning, online clothing sales took longer to grow.

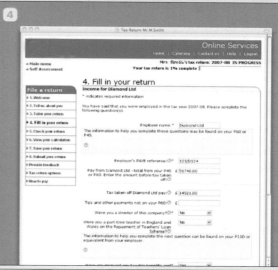

A Study the sentence on the right. Each phrase in box a could go in the space. What effect would each one have on the base meaning? Mark from *** = very confident to * = very tentative.

B Survey the text on the opposite page.
  1 What will the text be about?
  2 Write three research questions.

C Read the text. Does it answer your questions?

D Answer these questions.
  1 According to what criteria can we group factors affecting e-commerce penetration?
  2 Under what heading could we categorize consumers' perception of quality?
  3 What can local government do to contribute to the development of e-commerce?
  4 Is the level of physical infrastructure development in a country likely to affect e-commerce in goods and services equally?
  5 What legislation might improve e-commerce penetration, according to the article?
  6 What benefits can e-government deliver, according to the article?

E Find the phrases in box b in the text. Is the writer *confident* (**C**) or *tentative* (**T**) about the information which follows?

F Look at the writer's description of the government's role in the development of e-commerce in Singapore (paragraph 5).
  1 Underline the marked words.
  2 What does the choice of these words tell you about the writer's opinion of the government's actions?
  3 Find neutral words to use in their place.

G Study the example sentence on the right, and then sentences A and B.
  1 Divide sentences A and B into small parts, as in the example sentence.
  2 Underline any linking words (e.g., conjunctions).
  3 Find the subjects, verbs, objects/complements and adverbial phrases which go together.
  4 Make several short, simple sentences which show the meaning.

The redesign of our virtual shopfront

_____

the increase in sales.

---

a
probably caused _____

may have contributed to _____

was possibly one of the factors which contributed to _____

could have been a factor which led to

_____

caused _____

seems to have caused _____

---

b
The evidence indicates that ... _____

It is obvious ... _____

A recent survey has found ... _____

Most writers agree ... _____

Many writers seem to agree ... _____

The evidence suggests that ... _____

Their survey found ... _____

Example:

The availability of browser encryption | and | secure web servers | are usually thought of | as global factors, | while | national factors | include | both | the level of Internet penetration and its speed ...

A

Developments in technical infrastructure can often be carried out quickly, whereas other infrastructure developments, which require political intervention, take place over much longer timescales.

B

This data shows how, by implementing a technical infrastructure to put Singapore's regulatory frameworks online, the government could directly influence the take-up of e-commerce by businesses.

Overcoming barriers to e-commerce

E-commerce has tremendous potential to speed up, simplify and reduce the cost of all kinds of commercial and non-commercial transactions, and to provide easy access to global markets. However, the evidence indicates that there are significant barriers to e-commerce, resulting in huge variations between regions and countries. It is obvious, therefore, that by identifying these barriers and devising ways to overcome them, significant benefits can be delivered.

Bajaj and Leonard [1] have suggested that factors affecting e-commerce penetration can be grouped under three headings: culture, technology and policy. These factors can be further grouped in terms of whether they are global or local. A recent survey has found that the most important global cultural factor for international companies is ensuring that their e-commerce web interfaces appeal to different nationalities. Most writers agree that key local cultural factors include the level of trust between individuals, and also between individuals and their institutions. Technical factors can also be global and local. The availability of browser encryption and secure web servers are usually thought of as global factors, while national factors include the level of Internet penetration and its speed, which are both very low in many developing countries.

Many writers seem to agree that government legislation, such as setting targets for Internet connectivity and bandwidth, can have a significant effect on e-commerce penetration. In addition, government has a role to play at all levels. As Haag, Cummings and McCubbrey [2] point out, "Local, regional, and national governments can play a key role in promoting the adoption of e-commerce". Local and regional government can identify savings which e-commerce can provide in the delivery of public services, and highlight the benefits it can bring to businesses. Developments in technical infrastructure can often be carried out quickly, whereas other infrastructure developments, which require political intervention, take place over much longer timescales.

The evidence suggests that, in addition to the technical infrastructure, the legal, financial and physical aspects of a country's infrastructure also need to be considered. Roubiah, Hassanien and Khalil [3] assert that "well-developed legal and regulatory frameworks" are an important factor in the rapid adoption of e-commerce. Consumer protection legislation ensures that goods sold are good quality. The state of the physical infrastructure determines how far and at what cost goods can be delivered. Similarly, the state of the financial infrastructure will determine whether payments can be made quickly and securely. As Ou, Sia and Banerjee [4] point out, if trust in the quality of goods and services is low, there is likely to be less demand for online payment methods, as buyers may want to check their purchases before paying. The evidence from a BBC report [5] on China's e-commerce supports this position.

Let's look at an example of government intervention to improve infrastructure. In 2004, Teo and Ranganathan [6] examined e-commerce uptake among companies in Singapore, which already had a huge level of Internet penetration. Their survey found an astonishing level of e-commerce uptake among traditional 'bricks and mortar' companies. Much of this was due to the tremendous work by Singapore's government in promoting the benefits of e-commerce to these companies. During the 1990s, the government funded a gigantic e-commerce system for non-commercial transactions, allowing companies to submit import and export data. The system slashed transaction times dramatically from four days to around two minutes, demonstrating to business managers that e-commerce could be what Teo and Ranganathan [6] term a "strategic business decision and not just a technology decision." This data shows how, by implementing a technical infrastructure to bring e-commerce to Singapore's regulatory frameworks, the government could directly influence the take-up of e-commerce by businesses.

A Read the three essay questions. What types of essay are they?

B Look at text A on the opposite page. Copy and complete Table 1.

C Look at text B on the opposite page. Copy and complete Table 2.

D Look again at the solutions in Exercise B (Table 1). What are their possible advantages and disadvantages for consumers?

E Read the title of essay 3 again.

  1 Make a plan for this essay.

  2 Write a topic sentence for each paragraph in the body of the essay.

  3 Write a concluding paragraph.

1 Compare the methods which can be used by governments to support the development of e-commerce.

2 Explain, with examples, how a company can use e-commerce to achieve a competitive advantage in its marketplace.

3 Describe, with some actual examples, the additional barriers which developing countries face on the uptake of e-commerce. Consider how governments can best solve these difficulties.

Table 1

Situation	
Problem	
Solutions	

Table 2

Solution	
Argument for	
Argument against	

A Expand these simple sentences. Add extra information. Use the ideas in Lesson 10.3.

  1 E-commerce has brought many benefits.

  2 Penetration of e-commerce has been very uneven.

  3 Technical infrastructure can be upgraded quickly.

  4 Developed countries have strong legal frameworks.

  5 'No-frills' airlines were quick to take advantage of the benefits of e-tickets.

B Look at text C on the opposite page. Copy and complete Tables 1–3.

C What do the abbreviations in the blue box mean?

D Look back at the text on page 81 (Lesson 10.2).

  1 Find all the direct quotations (e.g., Haag, Cummings and McCubbrey).

  2 What punctuation and formatting is used before and within each direct quote? Why?

  3 What phrases are used to introduce each direct quote? Why does the writer choose each phrase?

Table 1: *Referencing books*

Author(s)	Place	Publisher	Date

Table 2: *Referencing journals*

Name of journal	Pages	Volume

Table 3: *Referencing websites*

Retrieval date	URL

©   cf.   ed.   Ed(s).   et al.   ibid.   n.d.   no.   op. cit.   p.   pp.   rev.   suppl.   vol./Vol.

Case Study 1

Up to the early 1990s, travel agents sold airline tickets and passenger booking details were stored on computers shared between airlines. Older companies dominated the industry, and it was very difficult for new companies to compete. The growth of the Internet made the e-ticket possible. Details of bookings could be stored on an airline's computers and printed off the Internet by customers. Ryanair, a 'no-frills airline', used this as an opportunity to gain market share. By 2002, around 91% of its passengers had purchased e-tickets from its website, which it used as a marketing and promotion tool. It also increased profits by offering additional services such as car hire and accommodation. This innovative use of Internet technologies enabled the 'no-frills' airlines to increase sales while cutting costs. Ryanair's growth has been so spectacular that it has overtaken the older, larger airlines and is now the largest airline in Europe in terms of passenger numbers carried.

(Source: Oz, E. Management Information Systems. Cengage Learning, 2008.)

It is generally agreed that for e-commerce to grow quickly in a country, consumers need secure methods for making payments online.

In China, relatively few consumers have credit or debit cards. Despite the fact that e-commerce transactions are the quickest way to pay, evidence from Ou, Sia and Banerjee (2005) suggests that many consumers do not want to pay online. They have concerns about the quality of the goods they are ordering and whether they will arrive. By paying on delivery, they can check that the goods are as described and have not been damaged during transportation.

References

[1] A. Bajaj and L. N. K. Leonard, "The CPT framework: understanding the roles of culture, policy and technology in promoting ecommerce readiness," in *Problems and Perspectives in Management*, vol. 3, 2004, pp. 242–252.

[2] S. Haag, M. Cummings, and D. J. McCubbrey, *Management Information Systems for the Information Age*. New York: McGraw-Hill, 2002, p. 214

[3] K. Rouibah, A. E. Hassanien, and O. Khalil, *Emerging Markets and E-Commerce in Developing Economies*. Hershey, PA, USA: Idea Group Inc. (IGI), 2009.

[4] C. X. J. Ou, C. L. Sia, and P. K. Banerjee, "What is hampering online shopping in China?," in *Journal of Information Technology Management*, vol. 18, 2007, pp. 16–32.

[5] "China 'yet to embrace e-commerce'," BBC, Nov. 2005. [Online]. Available: http://news.bbc.co.uk/1/hi/business/4446278.stm. [Accessed: Dec. 3, 2009].

[6] T. S. H. Teo and C. Ranganathan, "Adopters and non-adopters of business-to-business electronic commerce in Singapore," in *Information & Management*, vol. 42, Dec. 2004, pp. 89–102.

Recognizing fixed phrases from e-commerce

Make sure you understand these key phrases from ICT.

'bricks and mortar'
commercial transactions
consumer to consumer
dispute resolution
e-commerce penetration

electronic commerce
goods and services
government legislation
non-commercial transactions
online payment methods

payment collection
regulatory framework
technical infrastructure
virtual storefronts

Recognizing fixed phrases from academic English (3)

Make sure you understand these key phrases from general academic English.

One of the …
In some circumstances, …
Even so, …
… , as follows: …
The writers assert/maintain/conclude/
assume/state/agree/suggest that …

In this sort of situation …
It is obvious/clear that …
It appears to be the case that …
The research/A survey found that …
Research has shown …
The evidence does not support this idea.

Recognizing levels of confidence in research or information

In an academic context, writers will usually indicate the level of confidence in information they are giving. There is a strong tendency also for writers to be tentative when stating facts.

Examples:

Being tentative	It appears to be the case that … This suggests that …
Being definite/confident	The evidence shows that … It is clear that …

Recognizing 'marked' words

Many common words in English are 'neutral', i.e., they do not imply any view on the part of the writer or speaker. However, there are often apparent synonyms which are 'marked'. They show attitude, or stance.

Examples:

Neutral	Marked
Online clothing sales **rose** by 10%.	Online clothing sales **soared** by 10%.

Soared implies that the writer thinks this is a particularly big or fast increase.

When you read a sentence, think: *Is this a neutral word, or is it a marked word? If it is marked, what does this tell me about the writer's attitude to the information?*

When you write a sentence, think: *Have I used neutral words or marked words? If I have used marked words, do they show my real attitude/the attitude of the original writer?*

Extend your vocabulary by learning marked words and their exact effect.

Examples:

Neutral	Marked
go up, rise, increase	soar, rocket
go down, fall, decrease	slump, plummet
say, state	assert, maintain, claim, argue, allege

Identifying the parts of a long sentence

Long sentences contain many separate parts. You must be able to recognize these parts to understand the sentence as a whole. Mark up a long sentence as follows:

- Locate the subjects, verbs and objects/complements by underlining the relevant nouns, verbs and adjectives.
- Put a dividing line:
  - at the end of a phrase which begins a sentence
  - before a phrase at the end of the sentence
  - between clauses
- Put brackets round extra pieces of information.

Example:

In recent years, many <u>writers</u> have <u>claimed</u> that there is a significant need for Internet <u>third-party payment systems</u> in <u>developing countries</u>, but the <u>evidence suggests</u> that <u>demand</u> for these systems is <u>low</u> and will remain so for a significant period of time.

In recent years, | many writers have claimed | that there is a significant need | for Internet third-party payment systems | in developing countries, | but | the evidence suggests | that demand for these systems | is low | and will remain so | (for a significant period of time).

Constructing a long sentence

Begin with a very simple SV(O)(C)(A) sentence and then add extra information.

Example:

	national governments		can help		
As many recent case studies have shown,	*national governments*	*in every part of the world*	*can help*	*promote e-commerce*	*in many different ways.*

Writing a bibliography/reference list

The IEEE* style is the most common in computer science and information technology. Information should be given as shown in the following source references for a book, an Internet article and a journal article. The final list should be preceded by a number indicating the order in which the items appear in the text. See the reference list on page 83 for a model.

Author	Title of book	Place of publication	Publisher	Date
J. Close	*E-Commerce Essentials.*	London:	Allan & Unwin,	1999.

Author	Title of Internet article	Date (or 'n.d.')	Full URL	Date of retrieval
BBC.	"PayPal to block unsafe browsers"	2007.	http://news.bbc.co.uk/1/hi/7354539.stm	Available: [Accessed: June 2008]

Author	Title of article	Title of journal	Volume and page numbers	Date
A. Molla and P. S. Licker	"E-government and e-commerce, partners or rivals?"	*Journal of International Electronic Commerce*	vol. *52*, 61–69,	2008.

*Institute of Electrical and Electronics Engineers

More information on referencing (including other systems such as APA and MLA) can be found at: http://libguides.murdoch.edu.au/IEEE or http://owl.english.purdue.edu/owl/section/2

11 COMPUTING AND ETHICS

11.1 Vocabulary · linking ideas

A Look at the pictures on the opposite page.

1 Match each picture A–D to a label. What does each item do?

2 What benefits can it deliver?

3 How might it be harmful?

B Look at the words at the bottom of the spidergram on the opposite page. Put the words in the correct spaces.

C Study the linking words and phrases in box a.

1 Put them into two groups for:
   a discussing reasons and results
   b building an argument

2 Is each linking word used to join ideas:
   a within a sentence?
   b between sentences?

3 Can you think of similar linking words?

4 Put the linking words in 1b in a suitable order to list points in support of an argument.

D Study the words in box b.

1 Are the words nouns, verbs or adjectives?

2 What is the stress pattern of each word?

3 What other words or phrases have the same meaning?

E 🎧 Listen to a recording about computer ethics. Check what you have heard against the text on the right.

1 Complete each space with a word or phrase from box a or box b. Change the form if necessary.

2 Can you think of other words or phrases with the same meaning as the underlined words?

3 Match the phrases below from the text on the right with a later phrase that refers back to them.

1	computer professionals ☐	a	death
2	loss of life ☐	b	employee
3	environmental ☐ contamination	c	failure in standards
4	negligence ☐	d	destruction
5	conflict of opinion ☐	e	disagreement
6	computer professional ☐	f	IT contractors

F Do the general knowledge quiz on the opposite page.

---

a

another point is   as a result   because
finally   firstly   for example   in addition
moreover   one result of this is
secondly   since   so

b

beneficial   censorship   conflict   ethical
faulty   harmful   impact   implication
justify   negligence   obligation
reputation   responsible   surveillance

Computer ethics

Computers play an <u>increasingly</u> important role in our society. _____ is that decisions made by computer professionals have an _____ on a growing number of people. _____, IT contractors need to <u>balance</u> their clients' demands with their <u>obligations</u> to society.

_____ to ethical reasons for this, there are also <u>practical</u> reasons why this is necessary.

_____, errors in the design or construction of IT systems can have <u>profound</u> economic or human <u>consequences</u>. _____, Bynum, 2004, refers to a chemical company, Chemco, where faulty computer system design was _____ for an explosion which <u>resulted in</u> significant loss of life and <u>widespread</u> environmental contamination. Because the system design was flawed, the designer's professional _____ was at risk. _____, if found responsible for the death and destruction because of negligence, he faced a large fine or imprisonment. This example of a failure in standards <u>illustrates</u> the importance of making decisions based on sound principles which can be justified.

_____, a conflict of opinion can <u>arise</u> between a computer professional and his or her employer. The employee may have a <u>disagreement</u> about whether his or her work is being put to beneficial or _____ uses. One _____ of this could be the construction, maintenance or operation of systems for surveillance or censorship. _____ it is <u>important</u> that professionals understand the ethical issues before entering into contracts.

Source: Adapted from T. W. Bynum, *Computer Ethics and Professional Responsibility*. Blackwell, 2004, pp. 60–86.

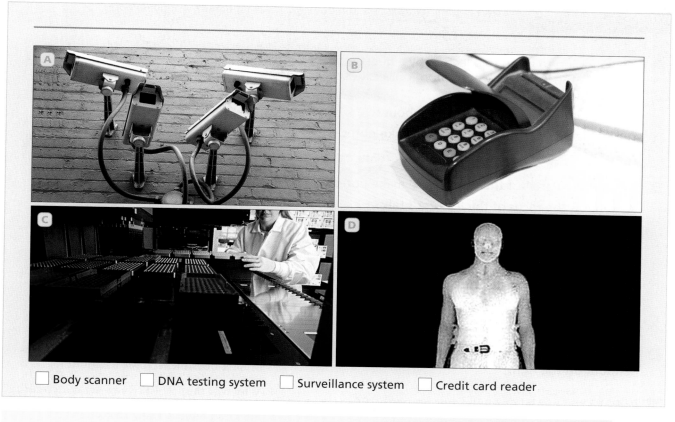

☐ Body scanner   ☐ DNA testing system   ☐ Surveillance system   ☐ Credit card reader

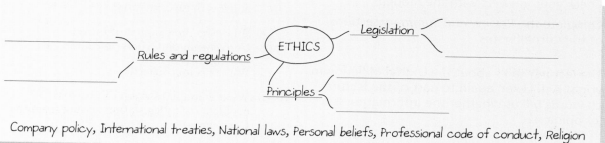

Company policy, International treaties, National laws, Personal beliefs, Professional code of conduct, Religion

---

🍁 **HADFORD** *University*

General Knowlege Quiz

1 Who or what are these?

a   Digital Millennium Copyright Act (DMCA)

b   European Union Copyright Directive (EUCD)

c   Computer Misuse Act

d   Hacker's Manifesto

e   UK Data Protection Act (DPA)

f   World Intellectual Property Organization (WIPO)

g   Digital rights management (DRM) software

2 What do these terms mean?

a   cybercrime

b   email forgery

c   keylogger

d   malware

e   hacker

f   Trojan

g   computer fraud

h   identity theft

i   phishing

j   botnet

A You are going to listen to a lecture by a guest speaker in the ICT Faculty at Hadford University. Look at the poster on the right.

  1 What is the lecture going to be about?

  2 Decide on how you are going to make notes. Prepare a page in your notebook.

B 🎧 Listen to Part 1 of the lecture and make notes.

  1 What is the focus of the lecturer's talk?

  2 What are the two main aspects that the lecturer will discuss?

  3 What examples of these aspects does he give?

  4 To which aspect does each example belong?

C 🎧 Listen to Part 2 of the lecture and make notes.

D Using your notes, answer the questions in the handout on the right.

E Refer to the model Cornell notes on page 104.

  1 Check your answers with the model.

  2 Complete the *Review* and *Summary* sections of the Cornell notes.

F 🎧 The lecturer talks about the Digital Millennium Copyright Act. Listen again to part of the lecture. Which words tell us whether the information is fact or opinion?

G 🎧 Study the phrases in the blue box. Which type of information below follows each phrase in the blue box? Listen to some sentences from the lecture.

  • restatement
  • definite point
  • summary of a source
  • example
  • statement of a topic
  • another point
  • tentative point
  • clarification
  • purpose for speaking

H Write out one section of your notes in complete sentences.

  See Skills bank

HADFORD *University*

Visiting Speaker: Dr W Mitchell
15th February 5.00 p.m.

'Ethics and computers: decision-making for the computing professional'

Dr Mitchell will explore key factors in ethical decision-making in today's rapidly changing environment.

---

1 Why were many Americans worried about the effects of computers in the 1960s?

2 What evidence was there to suggest that their fear was justified?

3 What examples of US government sources of data does the lecturer mention?

4 Why was the 1974 Privacy Act criticized?

5 How did the UK Data Protection Act address these criticisms?

6 Who was the Council of Europe Convention on Cybercrime aimed at?

7 Why was it criticized?

8 What example is given of possible problems with legislation arising from the Convention?

9 What types of contract does the speaker identify as relevant to computer professionals?

---

1 Don't misunderstand me …

2 To some degree …

3 It is fair to say that …

4 in an attempt to …

5 That is to say …

6 To the extent that …

7 Not only that, but …

8 … gives a good description of … in …

9 Briefly, (he) explains how …

10 (He) has no doubt that …

11 With respect to …

12 … is a case in point …

11.3 Extending skills

stress in phrases • building an argument

A Study the phrases in box a.

1 Mark the stressed syllables in each phrase.

2 🎧 Listen and check your answers.

3 Which phrases have adjective + noun? Which word has the stronger stress in these phrases?

B Look at the topics below.

- companies and the law
- justifying illegal activities
- ethical hacking

1 What would you like to know about these topics?

2 Prepare a page in your notebook to make some notes.

3 🎧 Listen to the final part of the lecture (Part 3) and make notes. If there is information which you miss, leave a space.

4 Compare your notes with someone else. Fill in any blank spaces.

C Answer the questions on the Hadford University handout, using your notes.

D Study the stages of building an argument (a–f) in box b.

1 Put the stages in an appropriate order.

2 Match each stage with a phrase from box c.

E Look at box b again.

1 🎧 Listen to a section from the lecture. Make notes on what the lecturer says for each stage of the argument (a–f).

2 Check your answers to Exercises D and E1.

F Use your notes to write 75–100 words about the main points in the final part of the lecture.

G In groups, discuss the research task set by the lecturer. Talk about these questions:

1 What are the three points in relation to hacking that you will need to consider?

2 Which one will you choose?

3 What ideas do you already have?

4 What kind of information will you need to find?

5 Where can you go to find more information?

Report back to the class on your discussion.
In Lesson 11.4 you will take part in a seminar on this topic.

a

disciplinary action
black hat
identity theft
denial of service
software exploit
social engineering
illegal activities
bulletin board

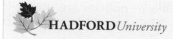 **HADFORD** *University*

1 What does the lecturer see as the purpose of company regulations?

2 What should Logistep employees have been able to do?

3 How did the BBC appear to break the law in 2009?

4 Why did the BBC avoid prosecution?

5 How does the lecturer describe *ethical hacking*?

6 What is your research task?

b

a giving a counter-argument
b giving your opinion
c stating the issue
d supporting the reason with evidence
e rejecting a counter-argument
f giving a reason for your opinion

c

It's quite clear that ...

But the question is ...

Research has shown that ...

I'm afraid that just isn't true.

Some computer professionals claim ...

Evidence to support this ...

A Study the terms in box a.

  1 Explain the meaning of the terms.

  2 Mark the main stress in each term.

B Study the words in box b. Match the words in columns 1 and 2 to make phrases.

C Study the InnerWeb Security Consultants intranet web page on the opposite page.

  1 What is the purpose of the page?

  2 Which guidelines or policies are shown in the pictures 1–3? Choose from the services listed.

D Study the phrases in box c.

  1 When would you use these phrases in a seminar and for what purpose?

  2 Which phrases can you use for linking your new point to a contribution by another speaker?

E 🎧 Listen to some students taking part in a seminar. They have been asked to discuss ethical hacking and some of the new techniques. While you listen, make a note of:

  1 the main topic of each extract

  2 further details of each topic

F Study the control panel for InnerWeb Security Consultants on the opposite page and discuss these questions.

  1 What is the purpose of this panel?

  2 What beneficial and harmful purposes could it be used for?

  3 What is the purpose of the screenshot control?

  4 Which controls have the least ethical implications?

G Discuss your research findings on ethical hacking with your group. One person from the group should report the conclusions of the discussion to the class.

---

a

black hat hacker
known software exploit
technical legal breach
password protection policy
Internet safety guidance
secure equipment disposal

---

b

1	2
client	testing
data	system
legal	access
penetration	protection
privacy	outcome
reverse	legislation
root	exploit
successful	engineering
target	consent
unpatched	situation

---

c

I'd like to start by explaining …

To carry on from this first point, I want secondly to look at …

I don't think that is the main reason.

That seems like a very good point X is making.

I'm going to expand the topic by mentioning …

On the other hand, you might want to say that …

As well as this issue, we can also look at a very different issue.

So to sum up, we can say that …

Does anybody have any opinions or anything they would like to add?

I think we need a different viewpoint.

OK, to continue then …

Following on from what X has said …

InnerWeb Security Consultants

Latest guidance and information on:

Internet use

- Employee Internet safety guidance
- Procedure for employee submission of unsafe sites for blocking
- Technical guidance on blocking unsafe sites
- Guidance on web monitoring of employees
- Guidance on employee e-mail monitoring
- Procedures for disciplinary action for inappropriate Internet use

Network security

- Password protection policy
- Guidelines for memory stick use
- Network security guidelines
- Anti-virus software

General security

- Building entry security
- Security audit checklist
- Secure equipment disposal

Employee Monitor

File   Logs   Controls   Options   Help

Employee Monitor

Programs Used
4 Program(s) Logged

Websites Visited
0 Website(s) Logged

Keystrokes Typed
1 Keystroke(s) Logged

User History
5 Action(s) Logged

Screenshots
2 Screenshot(s)

Control

Block Websites
Configure Website Filter

Block Programs
Configure Program Filter

User Settings
Configure User Options

Options

General
Startup and Access Settings

Logging Settings
Configure Logging Options

E-mail Log Delivery
Configure Remote Delivery

Current Status: Active

Linking words

We use linking words and phrases to join ideas together in a sequence, to show how the ideas are related.

Some linking words can be used to join independent and dependent clauses in a sentence:

Examples:

*The decisions made by computer professionals have an impact on large numbers of people **because** computers play an increasingly important role in society.*

OR

***Because** computers play an increasingly important role in society, the decisions made by computer professionals have an impact on large numbers of people.*

Other linking words join sentences in a text.

Example:

Computers play an increasingly important role in society. <u>As a result</u>, the decisions made by computer professionals have an impact on large numbers of people.

When building an argument, it is a good idea to use linking words to add points:

Examples:

Firstly, …　　　　　　　　　　　*In addition, …*
For example, …　　　　　　　　*Moreover, …*
Another point is …　　　　　　*… whereas …*
Secondly, …　　　　　　　　　*Finally, …*

Using words with similar meanings to refer back in a text

It is a good idea to learn several words with similar or related meanings. We often build cohesion in a text by using different words to refer back to something previously mentioned.

Examples:

First mention	Second mention	Third mention	Fourth mention
IT workers	computer professionals	those working in the IT industry	people in ICT
more …	rising numbers of …	growing …	increased …

Recognizing fixed phrases from academic English (3)

In Units 7 and 9, we learnt some key fixed phrases from general academic English. Here are some more to use when speaking.

Don't misunderstand me.　　　　　*The history of …*
I'm afraid that just isn't true.　　*The presence of …*
In an attempt to …　　　　　　　*There is a correlation between … and …*
… is a case in point …　　　　　*To some degree …*
Not only that, but …　　　　　　*To the extent that …*
Some people say …　　　　　　　*What's more …*
The effect of …　　　　　　　　*With respect to …*

Writing out notes in full

When making notes we use as few words as possible. This means that when we come to write up the notes, we need to pay attention to:

- the use of numbers and symbols for words and ideas, e.g.,
  Notes: (a) 'Big Brother' fears ⟶ Privacy Act 1974, govt. only - no commercial systems
  A result of these 'Big Brother' fears was the Privacy Act of 1974, which applied to government only and did not cover commercial systems …

- making sure the grammatical words are put back in, e.g.,
  Notes: ⟶ legislation copied by UK
  Later, this legislation **was** copied **by the** UK.

- making the implied meanings clear, e.g.,
  Notes: unauthorized access & crime ⟶ UK Computer Misuse Act, 1990
  Concerns about unauthorized access and crime **gave rise to the** UK Computer Misuse Act, 1990.

Building an argument

A common way to build an argument is:

1 First, state the issue:
   Does grey hat hacking help improve the levels of security in company systems?

2 Next, give a counter-argument:
   Ideally, there should be no reason to break the law by accessing computer systems without their owners' permission.

3 Then give your opinion:
   In fact, even white hat hackers can break the law at times.

4 Then give evidence for your opinion:
   The example of how grey hat hackers helped improve Apache security in 2000 provides evidence to support this position.

Linking to a previous point when your contribution is new

When you want to move the discussion in a new direction, introduce your comments with phrases such as:
Following on from what X said, I'd like to talk about …
I'm going to expand the topic by mentioning …
As well as (penetration testing), we can also look at a very different sort of issue.

Summarizing a source

When we talk about the ideas of other people in a lecture or a seminar, we often give a summary of the source in a sentence or two.

Examples:

A book by (name of writer) *called* (name of book) *published in* (year) *gives an explanation of how …*

Briefly, (name of writer) *explains how …*

An introduction to (topic) *can be found in* (name of writer).

12 ICT IN THE FUTURE

A Study the words in box a.

1 Find eight pairs of words connected in meaning. They can be different parts of speech.

2 Some of the words can be changed from noun to verb or verb to noun. Change the forms.

3 Check the stress and pronunciation.

B Read the headings of the texts on the opposite page.

1 What theme links the four texts together?

2 Read text A and look at the highlighted words. Connect each word to the noun it refers to.

Example:
They refers to previously mentioned noun *virtual worlds*.

C Study the verbs in box b. They can be used to introduce quotations or paraphrases/summaries.

1 Check the meanings of any words you don't know.

2 Which verbs have similar meanings?

3 Which verbs are **not** followed by *that*?

4 When can you use each verb?

Example:
accept = the writer (reluctantly) thinks this idea from someone else is true

D Read text B on the opposite page. Look at the highlighted sentences.

1 What is the purpose of each sentence?

Example:
Mirror worlds model the world … = statement of fact

2 In an assignment, should you refer to the highlighted sentences by **quoting directly** or **paraphrasing**?

3 Choose an appropriate introductory verb and write out each sentence as a direct quotation or a paraphrase. Add the source reference where necessary.

E Read each of the texts on the opposite page.

1 Identify services (such as Google Earth) which you use or know about, in each of the four categories covered by texts A–D.

2 Discuss which technology you find most useful and write a short summary of your conclusions.

a

anticipate   archive
augmentation   contingency
create   demonstrate   doubling
eventuality   geospatial   locate
mirror   prediction   produce
propose   reflect   revolutionize
show   stable   storage
suggest   transmit

b

accept   agree   argue   assert
cite   claim   concede
consider   contend   describe
disagree   dispute   emphasize
illustrate   indicate   insist   note
observe   point out
report   show   state   suggest

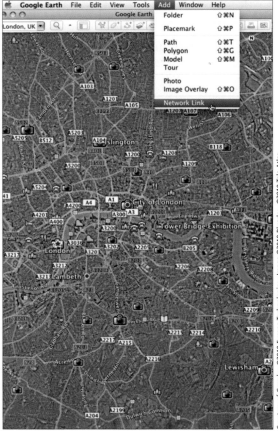

Courtesy of Google · ©2010 Europa Technologies · Image ©2010 Bluesky · ©2010 Tele Atlas

Virtual worlds

Virtual worlds offer an alternative reality, distinct from everyday life. They began as text-based role-playing games, whose players were mainly those with lots of time and a vivid imagination. As computer graphics improved, they made it possible to create detailed visual representations of the virtual worlds in which the games or role-plays take place. A common figure in almost all of these is the avatar. This can be a human or fantasy figure and represents a player within the virtual world. Two visions exist for the future development of virtual worlds. In the first vision all the activities of the real world can be carried out. Such a world can act as a platform for the provision of training and education, and for the delivery of services and customer assistance. The second is more limited. It is simply somewhere individuals can have fun interacting with other players in a variety of role-play activities.

S. Green and T. Ashley, "Exploring the future of virtual worlds," *Journal of Computer Interaction*, vol. 42, pp. 24–32, May 2008.

Predictive knowledge management using data from mirror worlds

page 429

Mirror worlds model the world around us, mirroring the geospatial reality that we experience in our everyday lives. They create an infrastructure which can capture, store, analyze and manage data which is spatially referenced to the Earth. Other data, such as the location of specific services or resources, can then be mapped onto these maps and images. An important role which has been proposed for mirror worlds is as a tool for managers to manage assets in the real world. It is clear that mirror worlds can play a key role in helping managers with contingency planning, so they can anticipate events, rather than reacting when they occur. However, it appears that the successful use of mirror worlds for contingency planning is very dependent on the quality of the data used. As Ding[1] (2009) states, it will be some time before it is possible to "look into a computer screen and see reality". Relatively low-cost GPS and camera technology, such as that used for Google Streetview, show how it is possible to capture large quantities of high-quality visual data quickly.

W. Chen, "Predictive knowledge management using data from mirror worlds," *Future Design Technologies*, vol. 14, pp. 429–450, Jan. 2010.

Exploring augmented reality

While mirror worlds make it possible for people to browse various types of information in a representation of the real world, augmented reality (AR) can bring that information to users in the real world. It does this by using a combination of GPS (Global Positioning Systems), and various hand-held or body-worn interfaces. Using GPS, relevant information can be found and displayed to the user. Existing mobile visual interfaces, such as touch phones, are already used to provide AR. By combining data from the built-in GPS and compass, they can map information onto images of a location, generated by the built-in camera. It is still too early to predict the full range of developments which AR is likely to generate.

B. A. Skelly, "Exploring augmented reality," *Journal of Mobile and Pervasive Computing*, vol. 24, pp. 239–245, Jan. 2009.

The growth of lifelogging

Lifelogging is the term used to describe the process where information on the location and status of people and objects is captured, stored and distributed automatically. By making information available in this way, it is possible for individuals to update others on their current status, to share news of unusual events with them and to preserve memories for themselves.

The drop in the cost of storage, processing and network connectivity, and the availability of ubiquitous computing devices such as touch phones, with the capacity to gather and store this information, has made lifelogging possible for a wide range of individuals. The type of information gathered can range from text notes, to streamed video footage from a mobile camera.

M. Richards, "The growth of lifelogging," *International Journal of Ubiquitous Computing*, vol. 32, pp. 349–387, Mar. 2010.

A Discuss the following questions.

  1 Why is the issue of growth rates for technical components particularly important for the future of computing?

  2 What factors other than components are important when considering the success of new developments?

B Survey the text on the opposite page. What will the text be about? Write three questions to which you would like answers.

C Read the text. Does it answer your questions?

D Number the sentences on the right 1–8 to show the order in which they happened.

E For each paragraph:

  1 Identify the topic sentence.

  2 Think of a suitable title.

F Look at the underlined words in the text. What do they refer back to?

G Study the highlighted words and phrases.

  1 What do they have in common?

  2 What linking words or phrases can you use to show:
- contrast?
- concession?
- result?
- reason?

  3 Write the sentences with the highlighted items again, using other linking words or phrases with similar meanings.

H Read the text on the right. A student has written about some of the issues associated with lifelogging, but some of the quotations and paraphrases have not been correctly done. Can you spot the mistakes and correct them?

I Using the information in the text on the right, write a paragraph for a university lecturer, summarizing how hardware growth has made it easier to capture and store data. Decide whether you should quote or paraphrase the material from the text.

	Twitter service begins.
	Google launches 1Gb e-mail.
	Steve Mann begins 'lifecasting'.
	Gordon Bell starts MyLifeBits.
1	Gordon Moore predicts a doubling of processing capacity every two years.
	Smart et al. make their predictions for the future of computing.
	Steve Mann creates the first wearable computer.
	Facebook extends its service to anybody over the age of 13.

As O'Brien and Ching[1] (2010) explain that the growth of lifelogging best reflects the increase in processing and storage capacity. For example, when Steve Mann created the first wearable computer in the early 1980s, it was extremely cumbersome p 59. According to O'Brien and Ching, they say that he was able to reduce the system to the size of a pair of sunglasses and was able to use it for 'lifecasting' details of his everyday life for others to access. This clearly shows the way in which hardware capacity growth "*revolutionized* the way in which data can be captured" p 59. When Gordon Bell started the MyLifeBits project in 1999, he aimed to capture and store as much data about him and his life as possible. He captured and stored e-mails, web pages, documents, recordings of meetings and photos shot at 60-second intervals.

Using technological growth curves to predict the future development of services

By M. O'Brien and T. Ching

THE RATE OF GROWTH in the processing power and capacity of computing hardware has remained relatively stable over the past 30 years. Popularly known as Moore's Law, the prediction made by Gordon Moore in 1965 that the number of transistors on a single chip would double every year has proved remarkably resilient. For example, the number of transistors on a standard chip in 1980 was 30,000, and by 2000, this had grown to 42 million. In real terms, that represented a doubling of processing power every 18 months. Another law, Kryder's Law, predicts that the capacity of hardware to store data will double every two years, and the growth curve has largely been in line with this. Memory capacity too has followed a similar exponential growth curve, as has the growth in bandwidth, both wired and wireless. Taken together, these growth curves add up to an exponential increase in the overall performance and capacity of computer systems.

A number of interesting predictions for ways in which this increased performance and capacity will be used are highlighted in a 2007 report by Smart et al. [1]. Drawing together current trends in existing Internet technologies, they identified those which could be used to create shared social spaces. These spaces would provide tools to allow individuals to interact with each other, and with the world around them, in ways which have not been possible before. They put forward three key developments as central to this future. The first was the development of mirror worlds, which would use online data to mirror the physical and spatial reality that we experience in our everyday lives. The second was augmented reality, in which this data would be mapped to the geographical location of an individual. The third was lifelogging, the capture and storage of data on events which relate to an individual's life.

Of the three key future developments identified by Smart et al. [1], it is perhaps the growth in lifelogging which best reflects the increase in processing power and storage capacity of hardware. In the early 1980s, Steve Mann created the first wearable computer (WearComp) to record details of his life. However, as the size and weight of WearComp made it extremely cumbersome, its functionality was very limited. So to increase this functionality, he began a process of development to make it smaller and more powerful. Although this took some time, eventually the wearable computer was reduced in size to where it resembled a pair of ordinary sunglasses. Consequently, in 1994, Mann was able to use the wearable computer for 'lifecasting', transmitting images of his everyday life to the Internet for others to access. This graphically demonstrates how the growth in hardware capacity revolutionized the way in which data could be captured. In 1999, Gordon Bell, a computer engineer and researcher, started the MyLifeBits project, which aimed to capture and store as much information about him and his life as possible. Initially, he stored e-mail, web pages and scanned documents, but as storage became more affordable, he began to record his conversations and archive them. He then began to store photographs taken every 60 seconds, using a specially developed camera which hung round his neck. Although he stores visual and audio data of all his encounters, this extreme lifelogging only takes up approximately 1Gb of storage space per month.

While extreme lifelogging is relatively rare, Sellen [2] argues convincingly that social networking sites are in fact "the emerging popularisation" of lifelogging. Social networking allows users to share data about their lives, using photos, music and video, as well as their thoughts and comments in text form. The growth of the social networking services appears to be linked closely with the fall in the cost of data storage. The rate of the fall can be seen in the landmark decision by Google in 2004 to provide 1Gb of storage as part of its free e-mail service. By 2006, this capacity had reached 2.7Gb, at the same time that the Facebook social networking service extended its free service to anybody over the age of 13. Social networking linked to video began to take shape around this time also, with the launch of YouTube in late 2005.

However, not all new developments will depend on the same technological growth. The Twitter service, which started in 2006, has been described as a form of social networking and micro-blogging. As it uses very short text messages, in contrast to other social networking services, Twitter requires relatively little processing power or storage capacity. As the key feature of Twitter is immediacy, it is possible to suggest that the rate of growth of service mirrors the number of individuals with mobile web access. The spectacular growth of Twitter, with up to 100 million users by the end of 2009, shows that while growth curves can be shown to influence new services, they are not very helpful in predicting them. While Moore's Law is likely to continue to remain true for some time to come, in one form or another, the shape of the services which will be developed in the near future are still to be revealed.

Future Computing, vol. 22(7), p. 59, 2010

A Study the words in box a.

   1 Check the pronunciation and grammar.

   2 What are their meanings in a research report?

conduct   data   discussion
findings   implication   interview
interviewee   interviewer   limitation
method   questionnaire   random
recommendation   research question
respondent   results   sample
survey   undertake

B Read the two *Method* paragraphs on the right.

   1 Copy them into your notebook. Put the verbs in brackets in the correct form.

   2 Identify the original research questions, the research methods and other important information.

C What are the sections of a research report? What order should they go in?

D Read the *Introduction* and *Conclusion* to Report A on the opposite page.

   1 Why was the report undertaken?

   2 What are the elements of a good introduction and conclusion?

Report A: Method

A written questionnaire (*design*) to measure how younger and older adults differ in their attitudes to new computer technologies. Six hundred questionnaires (*send*) to a random sample selected from each of the two subject groups, of which 250 (*return*). In addition, 25 young people (*interview*) in universities and libraries. Over 65% of the sample (*be*) male.

Report B: Method

Growth in the performance of processors is still in line with Moore's Law. In order to find out whether this rate of growth can continue, a literature search (*undertake*) using the Science Direct database and the Google search engine. The search terms which (*use*) were *growth curve*, *computing* and *processing*.

A Describe the data in Figures 1 and 2 from Report A.

B Look at the first paragraph from the *Findings* section of the report.

   1 Complete the spaces with quantity phrases. Put the verbs in the correct tense.

   2 Write another paragraph, using data from Figure 2.

C Look at the *literature search notes* on the opposite page. What issues do you think are the most important in encouraging older adults to see the benefits of new developments in computing? Discuss.

D Cover the *Conclusion* section on the opposite page.

   1 What should the report writer say in the *Conclusion*? Make some notes.

   2 Read the *Conclusion* again and compare.

Findings

Firstly, a _____ (20%) of older respondents (*state*) that they felt that new developments in computing would not be generally beneficial. In addition, the _____ (70%) (*say*) that they felt the developments would be generally beneficial, and a _____ (10%) had no opinion. The results from the sample of younger people were similar. A _____ (80%) (*indicate*) that they felt that new developments in computing would be generally beneficial, while a _____ (20%) of younger respondents (*feel*) the developments could be more harmful than beneficial.

Report A: Introduction

There has been much debate about the extent to which older people are excluded from the benefits of developments in computing technology. In order that all age groups can benefit equally from these improvements, it is important that older people feel positive about new developments and how they can benefit from them. This report will describe a survey undertaken to examine the differences in the perception of new computer technologies between younger and older adults. Recommendations will be made on how older adults can be encouraged to feel more positive about new technological developments.

Report A: Conclusion

To conclude, it is clear that there are a number of differences between the younger and older adults in terms of their perceptions of the benefits of new developments in computing. The evidence suggests that the issues identified should be taken into account when designing new computer devices and services. Older adults should be included in the groups used to test new prototypes, so that designs can take their requirements into account. In particular, these relate to the speed with which they can familiarize themselves with the product or service and the extent to which they feel control over it. More attention should also be given to publicizing the beneficial effects of new computer developments for older people. Unless these recommendations are put into practice, older adults will not fully realize the benefits of new developments in computing.

Report A

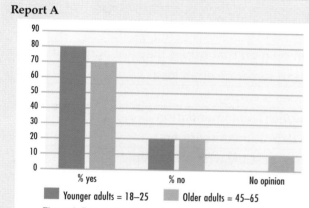

Figure 1: *Perception of new developments in computing as being beneficial to society generally*

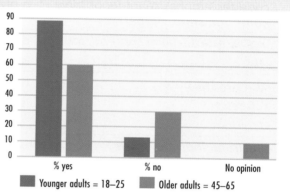

Figure 2: *Perception of new developments in computing as being beneficial to respondents' particular age range*

Report A

Literature search notes on issues relating to differences in perception of benefits in new developments in computing between younger and older adults

Issues identified	Context
1 familiarity with new computer technologies	more publicity for older adults highlighting the benefits of new technology; more free training courses would make it easier for older adults to use computers;
2 publicizing benefits of computing	older adults less likely to see information and publicity reflecting potential of new computer technologies; older adults need to be involved in the design of interfaces;
3 different age groups in design of interfaces	receiving training in using computer products helps users view computers generally more positively; extent to which adults use computers in their daily lives affects the extent to which they view computers favourably; different age groups have different needs in terms of design interfaces; interfaces may not be as intuitive for older adults;
4 more training for older adults	providing more detailed advice when purchasing electronic devices may help older adults use them more effectively; older people often have poorer eyesight.

Introductory verbs

Choosing the right introductory verb is important. Your choice of introductory verb shows what kind of statement the writer is making.

Example:
As Chen [insert ref no. in square brackets] *argues, the quality of the data used is very important when using mirror worlds for contingency planning.*

Your choice of introductory verb also shows what *you* think of another writer's ideas. This is an important part of academic work.

Example:
Skelly [insert ref no. in square brackets] *claims that the first commercial uses for AR will be found in tourist locations.*

Verb	The writer …
agree	thinks this idea from someone else is true
accept, concede	reluctantly thinks this idea from someone else is true
*consider, emphasize, note, observe, point out, state, suggest**	is giving his/her opinion
argue, assert, claim, contend, insist	is giving an opinion that others may not agree with
cite	is referring to someone else's ideas
disagree, dispute	thinks an idea is wrong
*suggest**	is giving his/her recommendation
describe	is giving a definition/description
illustrate, indicate, show	is explaining, possibly with an example
report	is giving research findings

suggest can have two meanings

Linking ideas in a text

Linking words, which join ideas within a sentence or between sentences, convey different meanings:

	Within sentences	**Between sentences**
Contrast	*but, whereas, while*	*However, In/By contrast, On the other hand*
Concession	*although, despite/ in spite of the fact that*	*However, At the same time, Nevertheless, Despite/In spite of + noun, Yet*
Result	*so, so that*	*So, As a result, Consequently, Therefore*
Reason	*because, since, as*	*Because of + noun, Owing to + noun, Due to + noun*

Referring to quantities and group sizes in a report

A/An	*overwhelming significant slight insignificant*	*majority*	
		minority	
		number	*(of + noun)*
Over		*half*	
More	*than*	*a quarter a third*	
Less		*x %*	

Structuring a research report

A research report is an account of some research which has been undertaken to find out about a situation or a phenomenon, e.g., *What do older age groups think about social networking sites?*

- Introduction   introduce topic; background information; reasons for research
- Methods   research questions; how research was carried out
- Findings/results   answers to research questions
- Discussion   issues arising from findings; limitations of research
- Conclusion   summary of main findings; implications; recommendations; possibilities for further research

Writing introductions and conclusions

Introduction

- Introduce the topic of the report.
- Say why the topic is important.
- Give background information.
- Give an outline of the report plan.

  Note: No substantial information; this belongs in the body of the report.

Conclusion

- Summarize the main points in the report without repeating unnecessarily.
- Make some concluding comments such as likely implications or recommendations.

  Note: No new information; all the main points should be in the body of the report.

Deciding when to quote and when to paraphrase

When referring to sources, you will need to decide whether to quote directly or to paraphrase/summarize.

- **Quote** when the writer's words are special or show a particularly clever use of language. This is often the case with strongly stated *definitions* or *opinions*.

- **Paraphrase/summarize** descriptions and factual information.

Incorporating quotations

- Use an introductory verb.
- Don't forget the quotation marks.
- Make the quote fit the grammar of the sentence.
- Show any missing words with '...'.

- Copy the original words exactly.
- Add emphasis with italics and write '[emphasis added]'.
- Add words which are not in the original but are necessary to fully understand the quotation out of context. Put the extra word(s) in brackets.

Do not quote more than one sentence **within the body** of a paragraph. If you want to quote two or three sentences, put in a colon and write the quote as indented text, so that it clearly stands out from the body of your essay.

However, think very carefully before you include a long quote. It is usually better to paraphrase in this case.

Additional material

5.4 Student A	**1 Secondary** = info from sources, e.g., books, Internet, trade mags., reports, etc. (i.e., already exists) + cheap; good overview of technologies and developments; relatively fast − journal articles → sometimes difficult to locate; poss. out of date

7.4 Student A	**Security** • Because source code is available to anyone, it is easier to quickly identify bugs and vulnerabilities in the software and to rectify them. It is also easier for hackers to identify weaknesses in the software. • Because upgrades to new versions of the software are free, it is more likely that open source systems will be kept up to date. • Because of its wider community of users, security issues are more likely to be identified quickly with open source programming. • Fewer computer viruses target open source programs.

5.4 Student B	**2 Primary** = new info: from (1) people, e.g., individuals using an interface; (2) experiment, e.g., research on network speeds under new loads + info = recent; specific to what you need − can be expensive; time-consuming

5.3 Symbols and abbreviations for notes

Symbols

&, +	and, plus
−	less, minus
±	plus or minus
=	is, equals, is the same as
≈	is approximately equivalent to
≠	is not, is not the same as, doesn't mean, does not equal, is different from
>	is greater than, is more than, is over
<	is less than
→	gives, produces, leads to, results in
←	is given by, is produced by, results from, comes from
↑	rises, increases, grows
↓	falls, decreases, declines
"	ditto (repeats text immediately above)
∴	therefore, so
∵	because, as, since
@	at
C	century, as in 20th C
§	paragraph
#	number, as in #1
?	this is doubtful

Abbreviations

e.g.	for example
c.	approximately, as in c.1900
cf.	compare
Ch.	chapter
co.	company
ed./eds	editor(s)
et al.	and the other people (used when referring to a book with more than two authors)
etc.	and all the rest
ff.	and the following as in p.10ff.
fig.	figure (used when giving a title to a drawing or table)
i.e.	that is, that means, in other words
ibid.	in the same place in the source already mentioned
NB	important
n.d.	no date given
No., no.	number
op. cit	in the source already mentioned
p.	page
pp.	pages, as in pp.1–10
re.	concerning
ref.	with reference to
viz.	namely
vol.	volume

11.2 Model Cornell notes

Review	Notes
	Legal factors: e.g., international treaties, government legislation, civil & contract law

Notes

Legal factors: e.g., international treaties, government legislation, civil & contract law

a) Privacy legislation in US
→ 'Big Brother' fears → Privacy Act 1974, govt. only – no commercial systems
→ response to increasing power of computers by mid-1960s & US govenment databases: tax, military, census, etc.
→ legislation copied by UK
→ Data Protection Act, 1984
→ unauthorized access & crime → UK Computer Misuse Act, 1990

b) Criminal & copyright/IP
Council of Europe Convention on Cybercrime
→ harmonize computer laws between countries
→ countries to investigate crime in other countries
→ different categories of computer crime

c) World Intellectual Property Organization treaties
→ implemented in US as Digital Millennium Copyright Act (DMCA)
→ prevents software avoiding DRM protection – controversial, not everybody agrees
→ implemented in EU as European Copyright Directive

d) Categories of cybercrime, e.g.,
data crimes → theft or modification of data
network crimes → preventing access or sabotaging
access crimes → gaining unauthorized access to system, introducing viruses, worms or other malware
related crimes → fraud, forgery, etc., using computer

e) contract law → covers employment and ∴ what computer professionals obliged to do
→ also contracts between companies/professionals where disgreement on quality of product or service
civil law → individuals can sue for breach of rights (e.g., damages suffered from defective product, invasion of privacy)
civil law → depends on country

Summary

104

7.4 Student B	**Cost** • Development costs of software can be lower because of code reuse. • Old versions of software can be supported indefinitely so there is no forced upgrade to new versions to ensure support. • Open source software typically requires lower specification hardware. • Higher levels of technical expertise may be required to maintain open source systems. • A wide range of free applications can be obtained for open source operating systems, although they may not be as sophisticated as proprietary software.

5.4 Student C	<u>3 Quantitative</u> = statistical info, often by carrying out experiments or through questionnaires + good for factual info; overview of trends ∴ large nos. − if looking at human-computer interaction sample must be big; results may ≠ reliable; low response rate for questionnaires

7.4 Student C	**Flexibility** • Openly available source code means it is much easier to transfer or 'port' the code to new platforms, i.e., convert it so it can be used on a different operating system. • Existing code can be 'forked' to develop different versions, e.g., both a stable release with basic features and a multi-featured, less stable, release for others. • New features can be added by users without having to consult with software owners. • Open source operating systems are more modular and provide more control over which features are installed.

5.4 Student D	4 Qualitative
	≠ numbers; usually verbal info; used to find out attitudes, beliefs, etc. Methods inc. interviews, focus groups, etc.
	+ reveal unknown probs; basis for quant. methods
	- in groups, opinions easily led by one person; only small numbers ∴ difficult to generalize

7.4 Student D	**Social**
	• Because source code can be reused, there is less waste of effort and the benefits of the software can be shared by many without further cost.
	• Greater democracy in terms of which features are developed in future versions.
	• Code is transparent, not 'black box', so it can be easily tested to ensure that software does what it is supposed to.
	• Cost is not a barrier to using open source software, bringing computing to a wider user base.
	• No limits on the distribution of open source software mean that good software is quickly recognized and widely used.

9.3 Human sciences-based usability testing methods

Task, user and environment analysis

In task analysis, the objective is to focus on the users' goals – what they want to achieve by using the interface, for example using a web interface to locate a particular service local to them. In order to understand how they approach this, it is necessary to understand the personal, social, and cultural characteristics the users bring to the goal. Task analysis also involves working out the specific tasks that users must complete in order to achieve their goal while using the interface. Depending on the results of the user analysis, the interface may need to be modified to take user characteristics into account, for example by using larger fonts for those with poor vision. A third type of analysis, which is often (but not always) carried out alongside the other two, is environment analysis, which involves understanding users' physical, social, cultural and technological environments. For example, one aspect of this might be examining the physical location in which a system is to be placed, to determine the type of light levels available for the visual display.

Focus groups

Although the focus group has its origins in marketing, it has become a useful tool for obtaining feedback on an interface at an early stage of development. Usually, a small group of around six users is asked to work with an interface. Under the guidance of a trained facilitator, they give their reactions to the interface. Depending on the stage of development of the interface, this may be a mock-up or a paper prototype (where the prototype has not been built, but exists on paper only). Occasionally, focus groups are used with working prototypes, for example where a device is very high profile and is expected to have a very wide appeal. Video recordings of the discussions are usually made so that exact quotations can be obtained, and key clips are sometimes put together to provide a summary of the session.

Cognitive walkthrough

Cognitive walkthrough is a method of testing the design of an interface at a relatively early stage of development. Expert evaluators use the specification of a prototype to create scenarios for various tasks and goals on the system. They then role-play the part of a user, 'walking through' the different tasks to determine whether there are any blocks which prevent the user from reaching their goal. If the sequence required to achieve a goal is very long and complicated, it can indicate that there is a need to review the action sequence and replace it with a simpler approach.

Thinking aloud

Thinking aloud is way of obtaining feedback from the user over the course of their interaction with an interface. A user is given various tasks to perform using the system interface. They are instructed to talk out loud as they perform the task, explaining what they are thinking about and the problems they encounter. The type of data gathered from this type of test can include:

- the users' feelings generally about the look and feel of the interface
- whether they like the colours
- how easy they find it to carry out the task they have been assigned
- what problems they encounter

This can provide very detailed in-depth data, but it is not always clear what users are talking about. By combining system logging and a record of the user's comments, this difficulty can be overcome.

Wordlist

Note: Where a word has more than one part of speech, this is indicated in brackets. The part of speech given is that of the word as it is used in the unit. So, for example, *advance* is listed as *advance (n)*, although it can also be a verb.

	Unit		Unit		Unit
A		billing	10	communication	1, 5
acceleration	9	binary	3	component	3, 4, 8
access (n and v)	4	biometric	3	complex (adj)	5
action sequence	9	black hat (hacker)	11	computer-assisted (or -aided)	2
active	6	blog	6	computerize	1, 4
adding machine	5	botnet	11	concept	7
addition	5	breakdown	8	confidentiality	11
adopt	10	'bricks and mortar'	10	conflict	11
advance (n)	5	broadband	4	connect	1
Ajax (Asynchronous Javascript and XML)	6	browse	1, 4	connectivity	10
analogue	5	browser	1	connector	1
analytical	5	bug (n)	1	consume	8
analyze	5	bulletin board	11	consumer protection	10
annotation tools	12	business to business (B2B)	10	consumer to consumer (C2C)	10
antivirus	1	business to consumer (B2C)	10	contingency planning	12
application	1			control (n, v and adj)	3
applications software	3	**C**		control unit (CU)	3
approach	9	cache	6	convention	6
arithmetic	5	calculate	5	convert	8
arithmetic logic unit (ALU)	3	call centre	2	copyright	11
archive	12	capability	6	core	5
assessment	4	capacity	8	cost	8
asynchronous	6	censorship	11	CPU board	8
augmentation	12	central processing unit (CPU)	3	creator	5
augmented reality	12	change	6	criminal law	11
aural data	9	chip (microchip)	5	cryptography	5
automated	3	chiller	8	current	5
avatar	12	civil law	11	cybercrime	11
		client	6	cycle (n)	3
		client consent	11		
B		cluster	8	**D**	
back end	7	code	5, 7	data	1
balance	8	cog	5	data centre	8
bandwidth	10	cognitive psychology	9	data integrity	8
barrier	10	cognitive systems	9	data processing	2
behaviour	9	cognitive walkthrough	9	data protection	11
beneficial	11	commercial	5,10	database	2, 4
'Big Brother'	11	common	8	decimal	5

Transcripts

Unit 1, Lesson 2, Exercise B 🎧 1.1

Part 1

Good morning, everyone, and welcome to the ICT faculty. I want to start by asking a simple question. What do the letters I-C-T stand for? That's a very simple question, isn't it? We all know the answer, don't we? Information and Communication Technology. But what is ICT about?

Well, if you ask most people to explain ICT to you, they will probably say it means 'computers'. So if I use my computer to play a game of Solitaire, is that ICT? Not really. It uses a computer, certainly, and computers are often found in an ICT environment, but a computer is a component rather than the whole system. It's an important component, as it's the part that processes data. But ICT is more than just using computers.

Perhaps if we look at the intrinsic meaning of the three words that make up Information and Communication Technology – three words that are used separately and together on an everyday basis – we might get closer to understanding.

Unit 1, Lesson 2, Exercise C 🎧 1.2

Part 2

Many words have an intrinsic, or basic, meaning. We might use the same word in different situations with different surface meanings, but the intrinsic meaning remains the same. Let's take an example, the word *virus*. It comes from the Latin word for poison and means a small organism that causes disease, and sometimes death, in living things. Is there any connection between that definition and the way that the word is used in ICT? Well, yes, there is. A computer virus is a program or a piece of code that stops a computer working normally. So we can easily see the link here.

As we learn our first language, we also acquire a feeling for the basic meaning of words. This helps us to understand the same word when it's used in a new context. So when we're learning another language, we have to remember to look for the basic meaning of a word because the direct translation in one context may not be the correct translation in another. For example, can you use the word in your language for *driver* in the context of *printer driver*, meaning the program routine which enables a computer to use a printer? The ability to look for the basic meaning

of words is especially important in the field of ICT, which is evolving on a daily basis and needs new words to describe new concepts, methods and applications.

Knowing the intrinsic meaning of a word might not help you to understand the exact meaning when you come across the word in a new context, but it can be a good guide. Let's have another look at the word *virus*. You may know the word because you were ill and the doctor told you that you had a virus. However, even someone who doesn't use computers, or knows nothing at all about computer programs, can guess that when someone says 'My computer's got a virus,' it isn't a positive thing.

Unit 1, Lesson 2, Exercise D 🎧 1.3

Part 3

Let me go back to my original question: What is ICT? Well, let's take some time to think about how and when we use ICT. ICT plays a huge part in all aspects of our lives. We use it at home, in schools and universities, and in hospitals. Most modern-day business and commerce couldn't function without some form of ICT, and industry is becoming increasingly dependent on information and communication technology to produce goods.

So what is the connection between a car assembly line, an accountancy software package, a computer game, or using the Internet to research an essay you have to write for me, or sending a text message to your friend to arrange a game of football? How do we use these examples to define ICT?

Unit 1, Lesson 2, Exercise E 🎧 1.4

Part 4

Let's look at the intrinsic meaning of our original three words: information, communication and technology. OK. *Technology* means the tools and machines we use to solve problems or do things efficiently. *Information* refers to facts about someone or something. In the context of ICT, information is data that is input, stored, processed or transmitted. That information can be represented in different forms, for example as a list, a text document, a spreadsheet, a picture, or an audio or video file. So what sort of information are we talking about? Well, examples include patient records on a hospital database, a web page advertising a new product, or the information that is stored in your car's GPS system that gives you directions and tells you when you've gone the wrong way.

Now, let's turn to communication. *Communication* means sharing information with others. So how does ICT help us do this? Well, there's a whole range of ways that many of us take for granted now. Some methods involve 'real-time' communication such as telephones, mobile phones, teleconferencing, and Internet chat programs. Non real-time communication methods include fax, e-mail or voice mail.

So ICT is about using technology to input, store, process and produce information, and about communicating this information to others.

Unit 1, Lesson 3, Exercise E 🎧 1.5

Introduction 1

In today's session, we're going to look at ICT in business. We will be looking at a car manufacturing company and discussing four areas of business: administration, finance, research and development, and operations, to see what happens in each area and how ICT supports workers in these areas.

Introduction 2

In this lecture, we're going to look at computer bugs. In general English, a bug is a very small insect, and there's a popular story that the first time the term was used in connection with computers was in 1945, when a small insect crawled into a computer, causing it to fail. Today, when we talk about computer bugs, we don't mean insects; we mean a flaw or fault in a computer program. I'm going to look at the causes of computer bugs and the effects.

Introduction 3

OK. Are we all ready? Right, I'll begin. Today's topic is the information systems life cycle. Systems development projects usually involve a number of people, often working in different locations. For a project to succeed, the goals and the procedures needed to achieve those goals need to be understood. There are many different development processes. Today we're going to look at the five stages that make up the *waterfall model*.

Introduction 4

The Internet, as we know it today, is a global computer network which connects millions of people around the world. This week, I'm going to talk about the origins of the Internet. Who were the pioneers? When did it all begin? We could say that it really began in the early 1990s, when Tim Berners-Lee developed the concept of the world wide web. But, in reality, it started in 1957, with the launch of Sputnik 1.

Introduction 5

The subject of today's lecture is CMC, computer-mediated communication. We'll begin by looking at one particular form of CMC, electronic mail, or *e-mail* as it is more commonly called. In next week's session, we'll see how e-mail works, but today we'll look at what we mean by e-mail and discuss the advantages and disadvantages of e-mail as a form of communication.

Unit 1, Lesson 4, Exercise D

Lecture 1 🎧 1.6

By administration, we mean the arrangements and tasks that secure the day-to-day running of the company. This may include hiring and firing people, drawing up contracts for workers, making sure that the company follows health and safety regulations, arranging meetings, and organizing training courses. So, what role does ICT play in this? Well, companies may use the Internet to advertise for new staff, databases to store staff records, word-processing and desktop publishing packages to draw up company documentation, e-mail to communicate with employees, or an intranet to set up online training.

ICT is also used to manage the company's finances. There are software packages to deal with payments and ensure that staff and suppliers get paid on time. These, combined with computerized banking, are a much faster way of handling payments than writing individual cheques. Specialized software is also used to monitor money coming in and going out and to analyze data that helps with decision-making.

In order for a car company to succeed, it must be able to keep providing products that customers want to buy, which means investing in researching and developing new ideas. Computer-assisted design – CAD – packages are used to produce new ideas and draw up plans for production. In some industries, simulators may be used to try out new ideas or to test a prototype product.

On the operations side of things, ICT is used in stock control, recording stock coming into the company and tracking that stock through the production process until the finished product is sent to the customer. It can also be used to reorder stock. Computer-assisted manufacturing – CAM – is a feature of many of today's car manufacturing companies, where some or all of the machines used in the production line are computerized. In some cases, a computer system will also control the production environment, for example where a product needs to be kept at a certain temperature.

Unit 1, Lesson 4, Exercise D

Lecture 2 🎧 1.7

So what are the causes of computer bugs? Well, bugs can occur in either a software program's source code or in its design, and they are usually a result of errors made by developers. For example, a programmer may have made a mistake when writing the source code, or the different parts of a program may interact in a way that wasn't predicted at the design stage.

The effects of a computer bug can be mildly inconvenient or they can be catastrophic. In some cases, you might not even realize a software program has a bug – this is because the bug has no effect, or a very minimal effect, on the program's functionality. In other cases, a bug may cause programs to crash – that is, stop working altogether. In such cases, the bug will result in considerable inconvenience to the user. Even more serious than this is the fact that bugs can cause security problems, laying a system open to viruses.

There have been a number of cases where computer bugs have had extremely serious consequences. In some cases, these have been financial. For example, a computer bug resulted in the loss of the billion-dollar Ariane 5 rocket in 1996. Fortunately, this didn't result in the loss of life. However, a software bug in the Therac-25, a radiation therapy machine, is thought to have led to a number of cancer patients being given overdoses of radiation between 1985 and 1987.

Unit 1, Lesson 4, Exercise D

Lecture 3 🎧 1.8

The term 'waterfall model' was coined by Winston Royce, a software engineering researcher, in 1970.

The waterfall model can be broken down into five basic units. The first stage is requirements specification. This is the stage when a systems analyst looks at an existing system, either manual or computerized, to see how things can be improved. At this point, the systems analyst will watch people using the system, collect information from users, and look at documentation. This will help him or her to identify the shortcomings of an existing system and produce a description of what the new system should do. The second stage is systems and software design. It is the responsibility of a software designer, or architect, to study the systems specifications and turn these into design documents for programmers to work from.

In the third stage, the development stage, a team of programmers creates the new software. Each programmer is allocated a part of the software to produce, so, although they are a team, they will be doing different things and progressing at different rates. For this reason, it isn't possible to test the system as a whole, so developers will test their own work as stand-alone units.

The fourth stage is integration and systems testing. When all of the separate parts of the system have been finished, it should be possible to integrate them – that means, fit them together, and test the system to see if everything works.

The final stage of the waterfall model is installation, operation and maintenance. At this point, the new system is installed and staff are trained to use it. From then on, the day-to-day running of the new system is the responsibility of the systems administrator.

Unit 1, Lesson 4, Exercise D

Lecture 4 🎧 1.9

Sputnik 1, the world's first artificial satellite, was launched by the Soviet Union in 1957 and marked the beginning of the 'Space Race' between the United States and the Soviet Union. Faced with losing the lead in military science and technology, the US government set up the Advanced Research Projects Agency, ARPA, in 1957. By 1969, ARPA had created ARPANET, a small network of computers in different cities which could communicate with each other. The technology behind ARPANET gave the US Department of Defense a method of communicating in the event of a nuclear attack, when normal methods of communication might not be feasible.

It rapidly became apparent that ARPANET could have other peace-time uses, and by 1972, scientists and academics around the US were using the system to exchange ideas and information. In

1973, ARPANET was extended to include the international community. The network continued to develop and by the early 1980s, the 'Internet' had grown to become a worldwide network of military, academic, and scientific research computers.

By 1986, the Internet was opening up to the general public. However, the real breakthrough that led to the Internet as we know it came when Tim Berners-Lee, a scientist working at CERN, a nuclear research facility, invented HTML, a computer language which made it easier to display text and images. He also invented HTTP, a reliable way of transferring information from computer to computer.

Since those early days, the Internet has continued to grow and grow. By September 2009, according to Internet usage statistics, there were over 1.7 billion people using the Internet, just over 25% of the world's population.

Unit 1, Lesson 4, Exercise D

Lecture 5 🎧 1.10

Electronic mail, or e-mail, is a way of sending and receiving messages in digital form via a computer. E-mails can be sent through an organization's internal communications network, known as an intranet, to which only members of the organization have access, or they can be sent through the Internet to anyone, anywhere in the world.

So what are the advantages of e-mail to the user? Well, firstly, compared to writing a letter, it's very easy. You simply type a message, add the e-mail address of the recipient, and press 'send'. And you can do all of this from your desk, or on the move using your laptop or mobile phone. Secondly, e-mail is a very fast way to communicate: in most cases, messages will arrive within minutes or sometimes seconds of being sent, whilst a letter may take several days to arrive. It's also comparatively cheap. You can attach large files with different formats such as documents, photos or video clips to an e-mail. Finally, by setting up an e-mail group, or typing multiple e-mail addresses into the address box, it's possible to send the same message to several people at the same time.

But of course, as with most things, there is a downside. Yes, e-mail is usually fast, but it's possible for an e-mail to get lost in the system and not arrive. Sending individual e-mails is cheap, but the set-up costs can be expensive: you need a computer and an Internet connection. There's also the problem of information overload – some businesspeople receive so many e-mails each day that they hardly have time to respond to them all – this may result in important e-mails going unnoticed. Another problem is 'spam' or 'junk e-mail'. This is e-mail that you haven't asked for but which is sent out to advertise products or services. However, possibly the biggest disadvantage of e-mail is that it can be used to introduce viruses to a computer – the virus can be sent as an e-mail attachment which activates itself when the attachment is opened, or it can be sent within the e-mail itself.

Unit 3, Lesson 2, Exercise B 🎧 1.11

Part 1

OK. Is everyone here? Good, then let's begin. We've seen how ICT is used in pretty much all areas of modern life – it helps us learn, do our work, communicate with other people, spend our leisure time, stay healthy and manage our day-to-day lives. We appreciate being able to watch satellite TV, buy groceries online and communicate with friends and family around the world. However, most people don't think about the technology that enables us to do these things. In today's lecture, we're going to look at ICT systems, specifically the different *types* of ICT systems, the *components* that make up an ICT system, and the *functions* that ICT systems perform.

There are basically two types of ICT systems: *embedded* and *general purpose*. We'll start with embedded systems. An embedded system is one which is fixed inside the device that it controls. I'll repeat that: embedded systems are found in all sorts of everyday devices, from the automated teller machine outside your bank, to the washing machine in your kitchen and the car in your garage. Embedded systems are special-purpose systems that are pre-programmed to perform specific tasks. There is a big advantage to these embedded systems. They are relatively inexpensive to produce because, unlike a PC or a laptop, they are designed to perform a limited set of tasks. In other words, embedded systems can only do one task or set of tasks.

Now let's have a look at general purpose systems. These are systems that can be set up to perform different tasks. They include supercomputers, mainframe computers and microcomputers. Think about your own laptop or PC. What are the different things you use your computer for? Well, you could use it to play games, produce assignments, watch films, listen to the radio or make phone calls. The list of things you can do with a general purpose computer is pretty extensive. This is because, unlike embedded systems, general purpose systems can be used for a whole range of things. Users can extend the range in a number of ways. They can reprogram them, upgrade them, add on new hardware, or install new software to increase the capabilities of the system.

OK, we've talked about types of systems that exist. Now let's think about the functions of ICT systems.

Unit 3, Lesson 2, Exercise C 🎧 1.12

Part 2

In the first part of this lecture, I defined ICT systems as two different types: embedded systems and general purpose systems. But they can also be defined in terms of what they do. Broadly speaking, ICT systems perform three functions. The first is *information storage and management*. For example, doctors often use information systems to store information about their patients. When a patient comes into the surgery, the doctor can call up their record from a database and see what problems and treatments the patient has had in the past.

The second function is *control*. What do control systems do? Well, an ICT control system is an electronic system which uses data to manage or regulate something; this could be a device or another system. An example of a control system is the one found in your washing machine. It's the system that allows you to wash clothes at different temperatures or use different programs by simply pressing a button.

Finally, we have *communications systems*, which transmit data from one place to another using a range of communication channels including telephone lines, cables and satellite. All kinds of data can be transmitted: not simply text documents, but also pictures, sound and video files. If you have a mobile phone, the chances are that not only can you speak to your friends on it and send text messages, you can also take and send pictures and short videos, pick up e-mails and listen to the radio.

Of course, nothing is straightforward, particularly in the world of ICT, and many ICT systems don't slot comfortably into just one category because they perform one or more functions. Many of us prefer to do our shopping online because it's more convenient and also because there's often more choice. A retail website lists information about what products are available for us to choose from. When an online order is placed, the system does a number of things. Firstly, this may be generating an instruction to prepare the products for dispatch; secondly, requesting payment from a credit card company or a bank; thirdly, sending an e-mail to the purchaser to confirm their order and, lastly, reordering new stock for the future. In this case, the system combines information management and communications.

So we have three types of function that can be carried out by ICT systems. In the next part of the lecture, we will consider the components of an ICT system.

Unit 3, Lesson 2, Exercise D 🎧 1.13

Part 3

ICT systems are composed of hardware, software, data and users. In this section, we're going to focus on hardware and software.

First, let's define what we mean by *hardware*. The word *hardware* refers to the physical components of an ICT system. ICT systems have four basic hardware components and these are input devices, processors, storage devices and output devices.

Input devices are the devices used to capture data. They include keyboards, microphones, digital cameras, scanners and devices such as mice, joysticks or touch screens. Next, we have the processor. This is the part of the system that controls the computer hardware and acts on the data that is put into the system. It's called a microprocessor or CPU – central processing unit. Storage devices are used to keep data that has been processed or will be processed at a later date. They include internal storage devices, such as RAM – random access memory – and hard drives, and external devices, such as flash drives or CDs. Finally, we have output devices such as printers or VDUs – visual display units – which are used to display or produce the results of processing.

Now let's have a look at *software*. Software can be defined as the instructions or programs that tell the hardware what to do with data. Software can be divided into two categories: systems software and applications software.

Systems software is the software that enables a system to work. It tells the system what to do and when to do it. Systems software includes operating systems, compilers, networking systems, performance monitoring software and utility programs. Applications software is what enables a user to do something specific with an ICT system, i.e., it allows you to do the things you want to do, whether that is designing a new product, organizing the day-to-day running of a company, or playing a computer game.

Unit 3, Lesson 2, Exercise E 🎧 1.14

Part 4

So, to summarize, we can say that there are two types of ICT system: embedded and general purpose. ICT systems can also be defined by what they do, for example information storage and management systems, control systems and communications systems. Systems are composed of hardware and software. The hardware refers to the physical components of the system, while the software is the instructions which control what the computer does.

OK, that's it for today. Next time we'll look at how ICT systems work. Don't forget to do a bit of research on that before you come. Thanks. See you soon.

Unit 3, Lesson 2, Exercise F 🎧 1.15

1 Embedded systems are not expensive to produce.
2 You can add new hardware and software onto an embedded system.
3 ICT systems can perform more than one function.
4 A personal computer is an example of an embedded system.
5 ICT systems have two basic hardware components.
6 Operating systems are examples of applications software.

Unit 3, Lesson 3, Exercise A 🎧 1.16

1 e'lectrical
2 'management
3 co'mmunicate
4 com'ponent
5 'storage
6 'binary
7 con'trol
8 infor'mation
9 em'bedded
10 'process
11 'database
12 'satellite
13 'automated
14 'function
15 'regulate
16 appli'cation
17 in'struction
18 'system

Unit 3, Lesson 4, Exercise C 🎧 1.17

Part 1

OK. In the last lecture, we talked about different types of ICT systems, the functions of ICT systems, and the different parts that make up an ICT system, i.e., software and hardware.

Today we're going to concentrate on what ICT systems do, and we can break this down into three stages: data capture, data processing and data output. But before we think about the different stages, it's important that you understand the difference between data and information. Data is information that has no meaning or context. For example, if you see the numbers 281204 written in a line, what do they mean? Well, it could be an important date, a price or a product code. We have no idea unless we have a context. This is data. If I tell you that 281207 is your course number, you have a context, and the numbers become information. Alternatively, if there was a small space between each pair of numbers, this could be a date – the 28th December, 2007. And if there was another set of numbers in brackets in front of this string, we might assume that it is a telephone number. So we can say that data + context = information. Information is data which has meaning, something we can use.

Unit 3, Lesson 4, Exercise D 🎧 1.18

Part 2

Right, let's have a look at the first stage now – data capture. We can also call data capture data input. *Input* simply means putting data into a system. So how do we do this? Well, data can exist in a number of forms, but all data that is input into a system, whatever its original form, has to be encoded. That means converted into a form that the system can store or process. Data, whether it is in the form of text, movement or sound, is stored as electrical signals which have one of two states, either *on* or *off*. The figure 1 is on, while the figure 0 is off. Each of these binary digits is called a *bit*.

Data that is input is then stored for later use, or processed. This is done by the microprocessor, also known as a CPU, or central processing unit. There are three parts to the CPU. These are the CU, or control unit, the ALU, which stands for arithmetic and logic unit, and the IAS, or immediate access store. The IAS holds data and programs which are needed for processing. The ALU performs calculations on data and the CU uses the results of these calculations, together with instructions held in its own data and programs, to make decisions about what to do with the calculations. For example, the calculations may be used to work out how much to pay employees in a company, or they may be used to switch on a system such as a central heating system.

Unit 3, Lesson 4, Exercise E 🎧 1.19

Part 3

Let's move on to output now. *Output* is what you get when a system has finished the processing stage. It is the result of data processing, which is then transmitted, or communicated, to the user. Output is the stage when data is decoded and once again becomes information which can be used by a person or another device. It might be a sound that alerts the police that someone is breaking into your house, a picture you can print out and display, or information about product sales that you can use to make decisions about the future of your company.

Some ICT systems operate as a cycle. A cycle is a continuous circle with no beginning and no end, although it can be broken if the system is switched off, or if there's a problem. In a cycle, the output produced is used as feedback to input more data into the system, which is then processed. One such system is the cruise control system found in many of today's cars. The system keeps the car travelling at a steady speed by increasing or decreasing the amount of fuel being fed into the car engine, depending on the input it receives.

Unit 5, Lesson 2, Exercise B 🎧 1.20

Part 1

Good morning, everyone. This morning we're going to learn about the early development of computing. In this first talk, I'm just going to give you an overview of the history of the computer up to the late 20th century, and then other key concepts will be dealt with in the next few lectures. Also, in your seminars and assignments, you'll be able to cover all the important points in more detail. So ... er ... let's see – yes – *to start with, we need to look back to* the early days of pre-mechanical computing. In other words, we'll examine the early inventions which led eventually to our modern computer. These were 'manual computers', that is to say computers which were worked by hand. The first manual computer was the abacus, which was in fact an extension of the fingers on the hand. The ten fingers are the basis of the decimal system, of course. Another important pre-mechanical invention was known as Napier's Bones. This was a series of rods which simplified and speeded up multiplication and division. Using the rods, it was possible to multiply numbers by using addition and to divide numbers using subtraction. *Secondly, I'll look at* the transformation to mechanical computing, whereby computers used gears and cogs to carry out calculations. These include the Pascaline, which was invented by Blaise Pascal in France in 1645 to calculate taxes, and the Difference Engine, which was devised by Babbage and is seen by many as the birth of modern computing. By the end of the 19th century, many of these principles were still being used in the tabulating machine, which used punched cards to process data from the US Census. The company making these machines later became IBM, which all of you will have heard of. *After that, I'll talk about* computing during the Second World War, particularly about the work of Alan Turing, an English scientist who devised a machine which could break German codes so that the English could read German military messages. The machine, known as Colossus, named after the noun 'colossus', which means a person or thing of great size, was built using electronic valves and relays. It worked very well and it was the world's first electronic computer. *Then I'll discuss* the development of electronic computers. These used transistors instead of valves, which greatly increased their performance and which would ultimately have a revolutionary effect on the speed and cost of computing. *I'll finish by mentioning* some of the factors which led to the growth of the Internet. These include the speed of development of different components used in the Internet and the particular requirements of communication in the Cold War.

Unit 5, Lesson 2, Exercise D 🎧 1.21

Part 2

The computer is arguably the most important piece of technology in modern society, but it actually has a very long history, in fact going back almost 5,000 years. It starts with the early Babylonians, who used simple arithmetic to count and keep a record of their goods. As their wealth grew and they had more and more goods to record, it follows that they would try to develop tools to make this work easier. A good example of one of these tools is the abacus, used as a basic calculator – in other words, a computer. What I mean is that, as in a computer, data is input by moving the beads. It is stored by the position of the beads and the output or answers can then be read off. Five beads per line are often used, just as there are five fingers on a hand. Anyway, moving ahead to the early 17th century, we find a different type of computer. While the abacus was developed to speed up addition, Napier's Bones were created to speed up multiplication. The Bones were a series of numbers written on narrow strips of material, originally bone, which allowed large numbers to be multiplied or divided using simple arithmetic. While they worked well, they appear to have initially been developed for academic rather than commercial use.

Commercial requirements were the reason for the development of one of the first mechanical calculators by Blaise Pascal, that's P-A-S-C-A-L, in France, in 1645. Called the Pascaline, it was a hand-powered adding machine which could add numbers up to eight figures long. It used gears and cogs to transfer the results of one wheel to another, a very simple and clever principle, which incidentally is still used today in electricity and gas meters.

There were quite a few more calculators invented after that, which I won't discuss here, because I want to look at another type of machine which was linked to the development of the computer. In 1801, Joseph-Marie Jacquard, that's J-A-C-Q-U-A-R-D, developed a very special type of weaving machine or loom, which was controlled by a set of cards with holes in them. Using these punch cards, the Jacquard Loom could produce fabrics with very intricate designs much more quickly and efficiently than by using traditional hand-weaving techniques. These cards introduced the principle of programmability, which meant changing the process by changing the input. This was very important to the development of modern computing and the punched card was to remain in use for well over 150 years.

By the early 19th century, more and more calculation was required to conduct government, commerce and engineering efficiently. Logarithmic tables, which allowed large numbers to be multiplied and divided using addition and subtraction, were increasingly used to speed up calculations. Charles Babbage, an English mathematician and philosopher, discovered many errors in existing tables and felt that the calculations should be carried out by machine for greater accuracy. He was given money by the British government to design such a machine. Unfortunately, the design for this machine, which was called the Difference Engine was very complex and the engineers making the parts were unable to manufacture them with enough precision to make it work. In addition, the government refused to continue providing the funds to allow him to overcome these barriers and as a result, his Difference Engine was never fully built as he designed it.

If the Difference Engine had been built as designed by Babbage, it would have worked perfectly. In 1991, a perfectly functioning Difference Engine was constructed from Babbage's original plans. As a result of his design, Babbage has been credited with inventing the first machine recognized as a modern computer, and so he is called the father of the computer by some people. In addition to the Difference Engine, he also designed an Analytical Engine, a much more complicated type of mechanical computer which would use punched cards to input programs to the machine and which would be powered by steam. Despite the fact that the Analytical Engine was never built, it had programs written for it – by a woman called Ada Lovelace. She is currently recognized as the world's first programmer and was honoured by having a programming language, Ada – that's A-D-A, named after her in 1983.

Incidentally, in addition to his work with computers, Babbage was also a cryptographer who worked for the British government. He broke – or decoded – a number of codes which had been considered unbreakable up until then, giving the British government considerable advantages in diplomacy and war. While this is the first time we find a link between computers and codes, it is not the last.

Unit 5, Lesson 2, Exercise E 🎧 1.22

Part 3

Anyway, er … to return to our story of the computer – we are now almost at the start of the 20th century, and the next important invention came from Herman Hollerith in the USA. He developed the Tabulating Machine to speed up the processing of information from the US Census, or population count. It used a combination of punched cards and mechanical gears, and it was very successful, reducing the time needed for data processing from eight years for the 1880 Census, to one year for the 1890 Census. Hollerith went on to develop more complex machines and started his own company which leased machines to governments and commercial organizations all around the world. The company which he founded eventually went on to become IBM, International Business Machines, which played a major role in the development of the modern computer.

Other developments were also taking place, which were more academic than commercial. Machines for calculating differential equations had been in use for some time. However, the Differential Analyzer, built in 1932 by a scientist called Bush from the Massachusetts Institute of Technology in the United States, was much more powerful and could perform large numbers of calculations much more quickly. The calculations were carried out using different sets of gears, making it an analogue device, similar to those designed by Babbage. However, it used electrical motors and, unlike Babbage's engines, it was not programmable and needed to be 'hard wired', that is, set up specifically for each new differential equation. The machine was successfully used during the Second World War to calculate the paths of missiles.

The Second World War also saw the creation of a machine which can be truly said to mark the start of the modern era of computing. This was a device called Colossus, developed by a British mathematician, Alan Turing, or T-U-R-I-N-G, in order to break German codes. It used electrical relays or valves to perform calculations and also to store some of the data while it was being processed. It was the first computer to do so, and because of this, it is regarded as the first electronic computer. Punched tape was used to input data and was a very fast way of doing so. Unfortunately, the whole project was kept completely secret until the 1970s, which meant that many people were not properly recognized for their discoveries during their lifetimes, which was a great pity. Er… Where was I? Oh yes. Once the first Colossus proved successful, a number of others followed, and by the end of the war, ten were in operation. By modern standards, Colossus machines were very large and slow, but by allowing the British to read German military communications, the impact which they had on the war was enormous.

Unit 5, Lesson 3, Exercise B 🎧 1.23

Part 4

Now, we have seen how important the role of computers was during the Second World War, but it was not long after the end of the war that the power of computing was turned towards business and administrative problems. The UNIVAC was the first American commercial computer. In addition, it was the first computer to be specifically designed for business rather than scientific purposes. Its calculations were performed using vacuum tubes and reading from magnetic tapes, a new technology which had been introduced for storing data. UNIVAC I used 5,200 vacuum tubes and weighed about 13 metric tons. It could perform around 2,000 operations per second. While vacuum tubes offered a significant advantage over mechanical computers, the technology was limited by cost, size and energy consumption in terms of how big computers could get. The development of the transistor by the American Telephone and Telegraph Corporation in 1947 showed a way around those limitations. Transistors could be made much more quickly and cheaply using a very simple and widely available ingredient, sand. In fact silicon, which is obtained from sand, is the material from which all modern electronic components are made. Transistors also consumed very little power and were very small compared to vacuum tubes. Computers which contained transistors instead of vacuum tubes could be smaller and still deliver as much, or more, processing power. With the arrival of the transistor-based computer, the modern era of computing had truly arrived. However … oh, dear … sadly, I see that we've run out of time. This means that I'll have to talk about the development of the Internet next time. In the meantime, I'd like you to do some research on what made it possible for the Internet to develop in the way it did. And before you get started with your research I want you to find out about primary, secondary, qualitative or quantitative research, and how each can help you with this task. We have looked at the development of computers up to the mid-20th century, so what I would like you to look at is the speed of development of the different components of computers, and the networks which link them together to make the Internet. We'll discuss what you've found out the next time I see you.

Unit 5, Lesson 3, Exercise C 🎧 1.24

1 crypt'ography
2 'digital
3 compu'tation
4 programma'bility
5 a'rithmetic
6 a'ddition
7 calcu'lation
8 me'chanical
9 tran'sistor
10 mag'netic
11 sub'traction
12 'chip

Unit 5, Lesson 3, Exercise D 🎧 1.25

The computer is arguably the most important piece of technology in modern society, but it actually has a very long history, in fact going back almost 5,000 years.

It starts with the early Babylonians, who used simple arithmetic to count and keep a record of their goods.

As their wealth grew and they had more and more goods to record, it follows that they would try to develop tools to make this work easier.

A good example of one of these tools is the abacus as a basic calculator – in other words a computer.

What I mean is that, as in a computer, data is input by moving the beads.

It is stored by the position of the beads and the output or answers can then be read off.

Five beads are often used just as there are five fingers on a hand.

Anyway, moving ahead to the early 17th century, we find a different type of computer.

Unit 5, Lesson 4, Exercise B 🎧 1.26

Extract 1

LECTURER: Right, Leila and Majed, what did you find out about the factors influencing the development of the Internet?

LEILA: Well, first of all, we talked to one of the computer technicians in the library.

MAJED: It's really cold in the library.

Extract 2

LECTURER: And what else did you do?

LEILA: We talked to the librarian. She was quite helpful and showed us some books which we used to get some data.

MAJED: That's rubbish. She was obviously really bored and didn't want to talk to us.

Extract 3

LECTURER: Leila, can you give us an explanation of your graph?

LEILA: Well, yes, it has a vertical and a horizontal axis: the horizontal axis represents time and the vertical axis speed and capacity. As you can see, we've put some of the different elements of computer components on it.

LECTURER: What do the rest of you make of this? Evie, what about you?

EVIE: Well, erm … I'm not sure really.

Extract 4

LECTURER: Majed, can you explain how you decided which components to include on your graph?

MAJED: Well, yes, it's based on information the technician told us.

JACK: So it's secondary.

Extract 5

LECTURER: What do you mean by 'secondary', Jack?

JACK: I mean it's an example of secondary research. They did two things – they asked someone for information and …

EVIE: [interrupting] Actually, that's primary.

Unit 5, Lesson 4, Exercise C 🎧 1.27

Extract 6

LECTURER: Let's go back to this graph for the moment to see how it can help with understanding the growth of the Internet. First of all, tell us about the components you chose.

LEILA: Well, the technician explained that components get faster or cheaper over time, or have more storage capacity. So we put speed and storage size on the same scale because we felt they were equally important. Isn't that correct Majed?

MAJED: Absolutely. There are other factors which are important too, but we felt that speed and capacity were the most important.

Extract 7

MAJED: The technician explained that, at first, hard disks were a specialized form of storage, so they were very expensive. Later disks were cheaper, even though they had less capacity to begin with.

JACK: Sorry, I don't follow. Could you possibly explain why that's important?

MAJED: Well, basically the cost of the product often depends on how many of them are being made at the time.

Extract 8

EVIE: I don't understand why the size of a hard drive should get smaller. Everything else gets faster or bigger.

LEILA: Well, as Majed explained, they were specialized. Those drives were used for the IBM 3340 and the number of drives manufactured was so small that they didn't have to worry so much about cost. Later, when cost became more important, it was cheaper to make drives with less capacity to begin with.

Extract 9

MAJED: Yes, especially when computer companies began to make smaller computers, for example PCs.

JACK: If I understand you correctly, you're saying that to begin with, the new desktop computers were much less powerful than the older computers.

MAJED: Yes, that's right.

Extract 10

LECTURER: This is all very interesting, isn't it?

EVIE: Yes, but if we just go back to the graph, we can see that apart from one fall in hard drive capacity, each of the components gets faster and larger.

LEILA: Correct!

Extract 11

MAJED: I'm not sure that's true. I think there may have been other falls which are not represented on the graph because the data is not detailed enough …

LEILA: I don't think I agree with that. In my opinion there is enough data on the graph to support our conclusion.

Unit 7, Lesson 2, Exercise B 🎧 1.28

Part 1

Good morning, everyone. What I'm going to talk about today is a key aspect of what makes computing possible – that is, the production of the software which makes computers work. In other words, how is the production of code managed? There are many different stages in the development of software, beginning with defining the problem. This includes requirements analysis, agreeing design specifications and system design. Of course, this can also involve building working prototypes for the client. The next stage is actually producing the software. This involves choosing a model for development, allocating resources such as programmers and computing facilities, and controlling the quality of what is produced. The final stage is documenting the program and troubleshooting any problems with it. Managing this whole process is also known as 'project management'. What I mean is … it covers everything relating to how the software is actually produced by programmers, and it can affect everything from what tools are used, how long the production takes, to the quality of the software. Anyway, we will look at project management later on.

So, er … in later lectures, we'll also go on to consider how developers approach the issue of balancing the costs of software and hardware when designing systems. Today, however, we will deal with general software production processes and methods.

Unit 7, Lesson 2, Exercise C 🎧 1.29

Part 2

As we have seen in earlier sessions, the computing process can be thought of as the input of data to the system, its processing by the computer hardware and its output. As we know, the speed or rate of processing is largely determined by the processor and memory available. Now, another term for the processor and memory is *system resources*, and a well-written piece of software makes the best possible use of the system resources. Computer software is also known as *code*, because it is written in specialized languages by trained programmers. Of course, as well as knowing how to write code, programmers have to know what they are writing it for; in other words the functional specification of the program. Once this is known, decisions on system design can be made. In this case, system design considerations will include the choice of operating system or platform it will run on, the type of back end or database technology which will be used, and what technical standards will be used by the front end. And then, finally, as we saw previously, once the system design decisions have been made, resource and scheduling issues will need to be considered.

Unit 7, Lesson 2, Exercise E 🎧 1.30

Part 3

Now, an important concept in software development is defining user requirements – the need to ensure that a statement of requirements is agreed with the client *before* any work starts. What do I mean by client requirements? Well, to help you understand this idea clearly, can you look for a moment at the leaflet I have given you from the Small Web Development Company? As you can see, the first stage is agreeing a statement of requirements, after which there are several stages before a decision is made on what web design will be produced. Looking at it another way, it is only when agreement has been reached with the client on the functionality of the software that the developers can begin to work. It is also important that the agreement on functionality is clearly documented, as otherwise problems can occur when more and more functionality is added to the project at the request of the client. In project management terms, this is called 'feature creep', where the project gets bigger and bigger as the client asks for more and more functions to be added to the software. When a web development company produces a number of mock-ups for a client, they are lowering the risk that the site which is put into production will not meet the client's requirements. Let's look at an example of this. Say the developers go ahead and build a website without taking into account all of the client's requirements. They show it to the client and he doesn't like it. The difference between the cost of the total development and the cost of developing a prototype is likely to be quite significant. Why is agreeing client requirements so important? Well, the point is that unless the developers know exactly what they have to do, then they can't choose the best development technologies or decide on a timescale which will deliver the project on time. In this way, resources can be allocated to enable the project to be delivered on time.

Unit 7, Lesson 2, Exercise F 🎧 1.31

Part 4

Now … er … let's see … oh dear, I see we're running short of time … but perhaps I should just say something about models used for developing software.

There are four main models which I will outline. To start with, model one is the *waterfall model*. In this type of model, each stage directly follows the other. It is called a waterfall model because each stage is dependent on the results which flow on from the previous stage. It is particularly useful for simple problems which can be clearly defined. The *iterative model* adds functionality in stages to software. Examples of this type of software are things like end-user applications or operating system versions. The first iteration usually provides the core functionality for the program, and each successive increment adds new functionality and fixes anything that hasn't worked properly in the previous iteration.

So the third model is called the *prototyping model*. What's important about prototyping is that clients have an opportunity to see a model before it is fully developed. It sometimes happens that clients are not totally sure what they want the software to do, but they feel they will recognize it when they see it. It is suitable for projects which are relatively small, such as website development. The web development company whose brochure we looked at uses this model. It means that full development only goes ahead when the client can see what the outcome will be. At the same time, the disadvantage, I think, of this system is that the design process can take much longer than with other models.

Lastly, there is the *spiral model*. What's different in the spiral model is that it combines elements of the waterfall and prototyping models. This means that the overall project is broken down into stages, as in the waterfall model. However, within each of these stages, the prototyping model is used to produce prototype software. The spiral model is particularly good for large, expensive and complicated projects.

Now … oh dear, I was going to mention the advantages and disadvantages of these models, but … ah … I see that time is moving on. So instead, I'm going to …

Unit 7, Lesson 3, Exercise A 🎧 2.1

1 'concept
2 de'pendent
3 'spiral
4 'increment
5 documen'tation
6 'prototype
7 re'quirements
8 'features
9 re'sources
10 pro'prietary
11 specifi'cation
12 functio'nality

Unit 7, Lesson 3, Exercise B 🎧 2.2

Part 5

I'm going to finish with some comments on the planning of software production – in other words, scheduling as a part of project management.

Now, the fact of the matter is, it's a highly complex task to plan software production. The reason for this is that planning decisions are based on a wide variety of different factors – not to mention the fact that some of these factors are totally outside the control of the developer. Let's take clients: a change in the client's company can cause a change in the software requirements, which of course the developer can't control. Plus there's the fact that the development model used for the software affects the way in which production can proceed, as we've just seen.

OK. Where was I? Oh, yes … So scheduling means working out what the different processes are, when they start, when they finish, et cetera, in relation to other processes. You've probably heard about Gantt charts? It was Henry Gantt who came up with a very simple idea to help with scheduling – the Gantt chart. Many organizations use Gantt charts to help with organizing and planning these types of software development projects. The advantage of Gantt charts is that they show what processes are happening at any one time. In a project which is based on the waterfall model, for example, work which is not ready in time can cause a delay in the start of the next phase. So, although it was in the early 1900s that Gantt invented his charts, they are still very much used today.

To sum up, then, production must be carefully planned. Let me put it another way … Planning must take into account the necessary processes and variables if the company is to succeed. Remember, poor planning causes project failure.

Oh, I almost forgot to mention your research topics. OK, what's very important in software development is the issue of whether software is open or closed source. So I'd like you to find out what are the main advantages and disadvantages of open source software.

Unit 7, Lesson 4, Exercise B 🎧 2.3

Extract 1

Now, as we know, the decision to make the source code of their products openly available is one of the most important decisions that software companies have to make. I asked you to look at the case of Netscape, a company which made the first successful Internet browser. Why did they do this? The product was very successful, and though it was free to individual users, it was generating a large amount of money from corporate customers. Also, there were many risks related to the decision. So, let's have some views.

Unit 7, Lesson 4, Exercise C 🎧 2.4

Extract 2

JACK: Well. I'd like to make two points. First, moving to open source was a move to defend their product.

LEILA: Can you expand on that, Jack?

JACK: Sure, Leila. Netscape was beginning to lose market share to Internet Explorer, at least partly because it was losing its technical advantage.

LEILA: So?

JACK: So the point is that by making their product open source, Netscape could include code which had been written for other open source projects. This would improve the product technically and would help them regain their technical advantage. So the point is that Netscape gained a huge advantage by making their product open source. Using code already written for other open source projects saved them time and money, because they didn't have to write everything themselves. And because the quality of the existing code was technically excellent, they improved their product very quickly.

LECTURER: OK. So, what's your second point, Jack?

JACK: I was coming to that! My second point is that Netscape wanted to provide the opportunity for developers outside their company to contribute code to the product.

LEILA: Yes, but there's no evidence that that would happen. If anything, programmers from Netscape were more likely to be involved in other open source projects.

MAJED: Well, I don't agree with that, Leila, because from what I've read, lots of people contribute to open source development programs.

EVIE: Sorry, but who are we talking about, exactly? People with good programming skills working in their bedrooms, or people employed by large software companies who work on these projects as part of their employment?

LEILA: Yes, we need to be clear here. It must be a mixture of both. Anyway, I'd just like to say that according to what I've read, open source products are becoming increasingly important for commercial companies.

EVIE: In what way?

Leila: Well, if you make your basic product open source, you can then provide a premium version which customers pay for. Also, you can charge users for support services which they may want to use if they don't have good in-house technical support.

EVIE: I don't get that. How can you charge for something if you are giving it away?

LEILA: What I'm trying to say is, some users may be happy with a basic product which they get for free. Others may want a more advanced product or they may need to buy in expertise for this particular software.

MAJED: I still don't understand. Can you give me an example, Leila?

LEILA: OK. Look at it this way. Companies which use a proprietary operating system for their servers, for example Windows, have to pay a fee for the software. If they use an open source operating system, such as Linux, they can get it for free. But their technical support may not be trained in using Linux, so they may need to buy in technical help while they are learning. So on the one hand, they may have to pay for support, but on the other,

they get the operating system free. And support is a lot cheaper than the system software.

MAJED: So the software developers make money by saving their customers money?

LECTURER: Absolutely. But it's not just about cost. In making a decision on which type of software to use, companies have to think about other issues such as security, how quickly the software becomes obsolete and how easy it is to modify it to their own needs.

MAJED: Yes, and I'd just like to say something else. As I mentioned before, lots of people help to write open source programs because they want to help other people. Open source can do a lot of good things for society in general too.

Unit 9, Lesson 2, Exercise B 🎧 2.5

Part 1

Good morning, everyone. I'm going to talk to you this morning about human–computer interaction, usually referred to as HCI. The purpose of HCI as a field of study is to optimize the performance of humans and computers together as a system. In particular, I'm going to talk about the two different components of HCI – namely, the human sciences and the computer sciences. I'm going to talk first about the human sciences, and I will outline some of the issues in psychology relevant to HCI. After I've described these, I will go on and do the same for the computing science components. I will also give you a summary of how they link together.

But before we begin I have a little story to tell you … I once spent six months working on a project, designing an interface for a new manufacturing system. It used state-of-the-art technology and made good use of colour graphics to show the operator what was happening with each of the machines on the production line. Sadly, when we came to rolling it out, we hit a major problem. On the factory floor, the operator had to wear protective clothing, with a special face mask which turned everything to black and white. He wanted to be able to use the interface without taking off the mask, which meant that he couldn't see the colour. Consequently, a lot of my six months' work was wasted. The point of the story is that it is really very important to consider all the human aspects when designing a user interface – in this case, the work environment. So … to get back to the main part of my lecture ...

Now, it's pretty clear that in order to be successful, system designers need to pay attention to the way in which users access information from a system. They also need to consider how they can enter data or give instructions to the system. In doing this, they can make use of a number of different tools and techniques. In fact, as we will see, system designers can adopt a number of methods to ensure high-quality interaction between users and the system. But I suppose the first point to note is that some of these tools are based on the human sciences and others are based on the computer sciences. It's the first of these that I'm going to focus on now, but I think it's important to point out that both types of tools are essential for good HCI design.

OK, so to start with let's take a few moments to consider the role of human sciences. What do we mean when we talk about the human sciences in relation to HCI? Well, research has shown that there are three important areas where human sciences can contribute to HCI. It could be argued that these three aspects also exist for the computer sciences. But as we shall see, they tend to have a different emphasis – I'll come back in a little while and tell you how they fit together.

The first important point to note here is that the human sciences can be used to build models of the ways in which humans interact with their environment, that is to say how an individual interacts with the world in general and with computers in particular. Its aim is to help system designers in developing the most effective interactions between users and systems. In addition to cognitive psychology, human sciences also draws on social disciplines such as sociology and organizational knowledge. From the point of view of system designers, it is fair to say that it is cognitive psychology which provides tools for detailed approaches to interface design. One example of this is the modelling of human input and output channels, a concept which is similar to input and output in computer systems. Examples of the human input channels are the visual channel which corresponds to the sense of seeing, the aural channel which corresponds to the sense of hearing, and the haptic channel which corresponds to the sense of touch.

Another area that modelling can help with is the type of metaphors which designers can use when designing an interface. One example of a metaphor commonly used is the folder icon to represent a storage area for files. The main aim of the metaphor is to help cut down the amount of time needed for the user to build a mental model of the system objects in their mind. By using tools such as cognitive walkthroughs, modelling can also

help identify likely points of failure for users when they are trying to navigate the system. Increasingly, we find that modelling is used to provide evaluative tools to measure the quality of system interactions from the point of view of the user. It's true to say that measuring user satisfaction in this way is a very important aspect of modelling. So, as we can see, modelling has been used to develop tools which can help with interface development and the evaluation of the user experience.

The second major point in relation to the role of cognitive psychology in HCI is its contribution to a simple model of how individuals interact with their environment. In terms of understanding how human cognition works, the Model Human Processor, or MHP, identifies three separate systems, namely, perceptual, cognitive and motor systems.

The perceptual system sends information to the cognitive system which is responsible for processing that information to enable people to know and understand their environment. The motor system is responsible for movement. This enables people to interact with the environment in response to their understanding of what is happening, based on the information they receive from the perceptual and cognitive systems. A simple example from everyday life, such as picking up an object, requires many complex interactions within and between the systems. For example, as part of the cognitive system, physical reactions in the eye which detect the colour and shape of objects. These then need to interact with the perceptual system, in order to make sense of what the object represents. In addition, each of these systems has limits to its capacity. George Miller, a cognitive psychologist, argued in his famous 1956 paper that working, or short-term memory is limited to holding between five and nine items of information at any one time. Miller referred to it as 'the magic number seven plus or minus two'. An understanding of these limits is crucial when designing user-friendly interfaces.

Thirdly, models of human interaction can provide very effective ways of approaching the design of interfaces, and of ensuring their quality. Used in an appropriate way, they can improve the usability of systems and considerably enhance the user experience. Crucially, they can be used to optimize the representation of tasks within the interface because they can help designers to understand how users view the world. By modelling the limitations of the various human systems, it is possible to ensure that the representations of the tasks will require the minimum amount of cognitive processing in order to interact with them.

A good example of this is helping users to remember options by grouping them together. As we have seen, seven plus or minus two puts a limit on what can be held in the short-term memory. Good user interface design incorporates this knowledge. Say an interface has 25 different icons. It is not possible for the user to remember all of these at the same time. However, the designer can group the icons by function to make – say – five different groups, each of which has a different function, such as formatting. The user then needs to remember in two stages – the first, to remember which group the icon is likely to be in, and the second to decide which icon is required. Bad design, on the other hand, ignores this types of knowledge. By arranging the 25 icons in no particular order, the user is likely to be confused and find it very difficult to remember where each one is.

Using these models will ensure that decisions are empirical, which is to say that they come from data obtained using techniques based on these models. So it should be clear that tools and techniques which draw on the human sciences are essential for system designers, and in particular for interface designers. On the other hand, it is also essential that tools which draw on the computer sciences are used and it is to those that we now turn.

Unit 9, Lesson 2, Exercise C 🎧 2.6

Part 2

Let's turn now to the contribution which the computer sciences, as opposed to the human sciences, can make to tools and processes in HCI. The main focus of HCI is on ways in which data input and output can be optimized, within the limits of system processing capacity. As we have seen in other lectures, system capacity depends on the specifications of the hardware and the efficiency of the software. Together, these will determine how much data can be input, processed and output at the same time. As we saw earlier, there is a significant overlap in the modelling of inputs, outputs and processing between the human sciences, and the way in which computer systems operate. The system limitations in a computer are similar to those in humans which are represented in the Model Human Processor. The most significant difference is that processing capacity and speeds in computer systems can be improved by increasing the specification of the hardware or enhancing the efficiency of the software, whereas of course, improvements in the human processor are difficult if not impossible.

The main focus of the computer sciences models of HCI is on how the system can become more effective within existing system constraints. Choosing the best combination of hardware and software for input and output devices is important if designers are to achieve this.

The speed with which feedback takes place is also very important, as it can affect the user's perception of the responsiveness of the device, and the ease of interactivity with the system. Again, choices on the specification of the input and output devices can affect this. For example, if display screens with a very high level resolution are used, high levels of system resources will be required to update this in response to user actions. Output devices which have a much lower resolution, on the other hand, will require much less processing power and can be updated more quickly, making them appear much more responsive to users. Because of the limits on processing power overall, the right choice of input and output devices can have an enormous impact on the quality of the user experience.

A good example of this is the Nintendo Wii and the innovative interface which it introduced to gaming consoles. Prior to the Wii, almost all consoles used controllers which were broadly similar. They were held in two hands and players used their thumbs to control actions within the game, using buttons or joysticks, and used their index fingers to pull triggers. It's tempting to assume that the designers felt that this design was ergonomically perfect and that no further innovation was possible.

However, in their approach to the Wii controller, Nintendo completely revolutionized the interactivity which was possible between users and the computer system. While it looks like a TV remote, the Wii controller can sense its position relative to the user and to the TV on which the game is played. This allows it to register speed and acceleration, as well as changes in direction, which makes it an ideal user-input device for games such as golf. Using the controller, the movements the player makes are converted into speed and movement data, which inputs into the game. Because of the intuitiveness and ease of use of its interface, the Wii became one of the most successful consoles ever, and expanded the market beyond traditional game players, to include families and older generations. So the real question is, why have other console makers remained with the traditional interfaces and what will be the effects of this?

Now, where was I? Oh yes, right, I was talking about how a system can become more effective within existing system constraints ... So what exactly have we looked at this morning? Well, to sum up, we can group the ways in which the human and computer sciences help us understand HCI under three main headings. Firstly, by providing models of an engineering approach to human behaviour, the human sciences can help us to understand the interaction between human and system in a way which can be used for planning and quality assurance. However, the human sciences approach goes further, taking into account the broader context of the interaction between the individual and the system. Secondly, by modelling human systems as channels, for example the visual channel, it is possible to determine the effect of changes in the input and output of a system. The third major point is the need to consider the effect of limitations on available processing in both human and computer systems. These differences and similarities between the two approaches are reflected in the different ways in which the usability of a system can be evaluated ...

Unit 9, Lesson 2, Exercise D 🎧 2.7

1 Well, research has shown that there are three important areas where human sciences can contribute to HCI.

2 It could be argued that these three aspects also exist for the computer sciences.

3 But as we shall see, they tend to have a different emphasis – I'll come back in a little while and tell you how they fit together.

4 From the point of view of system designers, it's fair to say that it is cognitive psychology which provides tools for detailed approaches to interface design.

5 Increasingly, we find that modelling is used to provide evaluative tools to measure the quality of system interactions from the point of view of the user.

6 It's true to say that measuring user satisfaction in this way is a very important aspect of modelling.

7 In terms of understanding how human cognition works, the Model Human Processor, or MHP, identifies three separate

systems, namely, perceptual, cognitive and motor systems.

8 So it should be clear that tools and techniques which draw on the human sciences are essential for system designers, and in particular for interface designers.

Unit 9, Lesson 3, Exercise A 🎧 2.8

1 'visual, 'input, de'sign, 'haptic, 'output

2 mental 'model, 'user input, visual di'splay, 'input device, 'action sequence

3 'actually, 'generally, 'usually, i'deally, 'crucially

Unit 9, Lesson 3, Exercise C 🎧 2.9

Part 3

OK, so moving on, ... Now, let's consider a question. How can we measure the effectiveness of the design tools? To do this, we need methods to test the usability of system interfaces. Just like the tools, the methods can be divided into two types – those which draw on the human sciences and those which draw on the computer sciences. Today I'm going to focus on three main evaluation tools which use the computer as a means of obtaining data on usability. These are *heuristic evaluation*, *system logging*, and *eye tracking*.

Let's begin then with heuristic evaluation which is perhaps the most commonly used method. A website called *useit.com* defines heuristic evaluation as "a method for finding the usability problems in a user interface design ... by judging its compliance with recognized usability principles, in other words, the heuristics." In practice, this involves a small group of evaluators, usually around six, each using a standard checklist to inspect the interface. They note down how each feature matches the items on the checklist. It's important that the evaluators work independently, so that they don't influence each other when making their judgements. However, their reports can be put together to provide one overall usability rating for the interface. This is a very simple method, but it can be a very powerful one. One possible drawback is that the method doesn't involve the use of the interface in the way it would be used in 'real life', so some aspects may be missed out.

By the way, I see that some of you are using the Cornell note-taking system. That's very good. Do you all know about this? No? Right, well, if you want to know more about it, I suggest you look at *How to study in college* by Walter Pauk, the 9th edition, published in 2007. It's very good, and it should be in the university library. I'm sure that you all know the importance of taking good notes – and this system is particularly useful.

The second computer-based method of testing the usability of an interface is system logging. Now, we already know that it's important to be able to identify exactly where problems occur in carrying out a task. System logging is particularly useful for this because it can provide actual data on the user's interactions with the interface. This means it can indicate whether or not an action sequence has led to the achievement of a goal. System logging can also show any tasks which the user was unable to complete. However, basic system logging does not identify the reason for failure. In fact, as Dix points out in *Human computer interaction*, one of your core texts – the 3rd edition, which was published in 2006, we can only rely on system logs to tell us what has happened, not necessarily why it has happened. A more advanced form of system logging is *video logging*. This creates a video of users' interactions with the interface, showing the actions of the user and how they tried to complete the task. While it can show how the user failed, it still doesn't provide the reason why – which could be two very similar icons, a confusing label or a hidden tab, for example.

The third method is eye tracking. This can be used along with a system logging method. It can provide even more detailed information on the user's behaviour as they interact with the interface. In eye tracking, the user is provided with a headset which can measure the point of gaze. This simply means where the individual is looking. We can use this device to gather data that can be collected on the point of gaze, which can show the choices a user considered before deciding on a particular action. This in turn gives a better understanding of the user's mental processes. Eye tracking can also be used separately from system logging, for example to determine how a user's attention is drawn to various parts of an interface. This can be used to identify distracting elements of interface design. Eye tracking can help bring us closer to what the user is thinking, as opposed to simply measuring their behaviour.

OK, so now we can see that these three different testing methods gather data on the usability of an interface, without actually asking users for information. In the first method, heuristic evaluation, the likely views of a user are represented by a checklist which an evaluator then uses to test the interface. In the second method, system logging, actual data on the user's behaviour as they interact with the interface is gathered. However, there is no data on what the user is thinking or how they feel as they are interacting with the interface. The data collected by the third method, eye tracking, covers the whole period of time the user is interacting with the interface, not just while they are trying to complete a task. This means that it can be used to give some indication of what the user is thinking during the interaction. However, while behaviour-based data is valuable, it must not be the only way of gathering usability information. To quote Dix from the same text as before, "analytic and informal techniques can and should be used".

Now I think that's all I'm going to say for the moment on the computer-based methods of usability evaluation. Are there any questions so far? (*Pause*) No, good. Now when I see you in tutorials, we'll look in more detail at the human sciences component of HCI. In the meantime, I'm going to set you a research task. Right, now listen carefully ... your task is to find out more about the methods of evaluating the usability of interfaces which draw on the human sciences. I'd like you to work in groups of four. Each group should find out about the various methods that are used and report back on your findings.

Unit 9, Lesson 3, Exercise D 🎧 2.10

Extract 1

Let's begin then with heuristic evaluation, which is perhaps the most commonly used method. A website called *useit.com* defines heuristic evaluation as "a method for finding the usability problems in a user interface design ... by judging its compliance with recognized usability principles in other words, the heuristics."

Extract 2

By the way, I see that some of you are using the Cornell note-taking system. That's very good. Do you all know about this? No? Right, well, if you want to know more about it, I suggest you look at *How to Study in College* by Walter Pauk, the 9th edition, published in 2007. It's very good, and it should be in the university library.

Extract 3

System logging can also show any tasks that the user was unable to complete. However, basic system logging does not identify the reason for failure. In fact, as Dix points out in *Human computer interaction,* one of your core texts – the 3rd edition, which was published in 2006, we can only rely on system logs to tell us what has happened, not necessarily why it has happened.

Extract 4

OK, so now we can see that these three different testing methods gather data on the usability of an interface, without actually asking users for information … However, while behaviour-based data is valuable, it must not be the only way of gathering usability information. To quote Dix, from the same text as before, "analytic and informal techniques can and should be used".

Unit 9, Lesson 4, Exercise C 🎧 2.11

Extract 1

It seems quite clear that computer-based methods can contribute a lot when evaluating the usability of an interface. From the point of view of system logging for example, there are three key points: firstly, it records users' actual behaviour, rather than what they think happened; secondly it can be used with many users at very little extra cost; and thirdly, pretty important this …

Extract 2

Erm, I think one big difference is the human sciences approach. This is very important. It is possible, we can see, how this is very important. So let's look at the slide and … oh sorry, that's the wrong slide, just a minute … right, so here is a difference between computer and human … er you can see I think, this difference … do you have any questions about this slide? …

Extract 3

We could ask the question: why would we want to use a psychologist? Usually this is very expensive, but it's necessary because a psychologist can help to provide a view of how the user will use the interface. In addition, a psychologist is also very important because they can show where the attention of a user will be directed in the interface.

Extract 4

So the main difference between the methods is the data. The human sciences-based methods provide us with data which is based on what the user thinks is happening. The computer-based methods can provide us with *actual* data on how the user is interacting with the system. This

difference shows us one of the main advantages of computer-based methods, although they are not enough on their own. In fact, if we look at the chart I've prepared here, we can see how the various methods relate to each other. For example, we can see that system logging can be used along with thinking aloud. This provides data on what the user is actually doing with the system …

Unit 11, Lesson 1, Exercise E 🎧 2.12

Computer ethics

Computers play an increasingly important role in our society. One result of this is that decisions made by computer professionals have an impact on a growing number of people. Moreover, IT contractors need to balance their clients' demands with their obligations to society. In addition to ethical reasons for this, there are also practical reasons why this is necessary.

Firstly, errors in the design or construction of IT systems can have profound economic or human consequences. For example, Bynum, 2004, refers to a chemical company, Chemco, where faulty computer system design was responsible for an explosion which resulted in significant loss of life and widespread environmental contamination. Because the system design was flawed, the designer's professional reputation was at risk. Furthermore, if found responsible for the death and destruction because of negligence, he faced a large fine or imprisonment. This example of a failure in standards illustrates the importance of making decisions based on sound principles which can be justified.

Secondly, a conflict of opinion can arise between a computer professional and his or her employer. The employee may have a disagreement about whether his or her work is being put to beneficial or harmful uses. One example of this could be the construction, maintenance or operation of systems for surveillance or censorship. So it is important that professionals understand the ethical issues before entering into contracts.

Unit 11, Lesson 2, Exercise B 🎧 2.13

Part 1

Good morning. My name is Dr William Mitchell and much of my work relates to computer ethics and professional responsibility. I am here today to give you an overview of issues you need to be aware of when making decisions in a professional capacity. That is to say, I'm going to look at ways in which you can justify your professional decisions.

Don't misunderstand me, I don't want you to assume that ethics are relevant only when making decisions in the workplace. As we all know, to some degree, ethical considerations will form a part of every decision you make in your life. However, it is fair to say that, in the workplace, computer professionals have to be careful that they can't be accused of negligence when designing or operating systems which have an effect on human life or property. Or, when developing software, that they aren't producing a product which is not up to professional standards or which infringes the legal rights of copyright holders.

So in an attempt to keep the discussion on professional responsibility reasonably simple, I'm going to summarize a few of the more interesting points to do with the legal and regulatory aspects of professional decision-making in a work context.

Unit 11, Lesson 2, Exercise C 🎧 2.14

Part 2

To start with, then, let's look at the different types of law which computer professionals need to be aware of. These fall into two main categories – national laws and international laws. It is particularly important for computer professionals to have a good knowledge of which laws are relevant, because they can then be clear about when they are within the law or when they are at risk of breaking it. If their activities can be seen as breaking the law, then they will need to be in a position to justify their actions. They may defend themselves by using the principle of the 'greatest good' – stating that more people will benefit from their actions than will suffer from them. Or they may want to rely on their personal beliefs and principles of what is right or wrong. Either way, it is important that they have a knowledge of the different categories of law which can affect their decision-making.

Well, first let's look at national legislation, passed by countries in response to aspects of computing which were seen as harmful or problematic. The passing of privacy laws in the US is a good example of this. By the 1960s, computers had become sufficiently powerful for many US citizens to begin to see them as a potential danger. The greatest fear initially was of a 'Big Brother' society, that is to say a society in which the government would know everything about its citizens and could exercise total control over them. By the early 1960s – and this may surprise many of you – the US government had already created a number of large databases containing data from the US census, from tax payments, from military service records and a range of other sources. By combining all this information, the government could create a very detailed picture of every individual's activities, giving the government unprecedented power over its citizens.

Public concern regarding government use of information from citizens grew to the extent that the Privacy Act was passed in 1974. The Act was criticized, however, because it was difficult to enforce and, not only that, but because it excluded the collection of data by companies and organizations other than government. Daniel Solove gives a good description of the issues around this in his 2004 book on technology and privacy in the information age. Briefly, in his chapter on information privacy law, he explains how the many exemptions and loopholes in the Act meant that it did not fully address the concerns which had led to it being passed.

However, it is fair to say that legislation in other countries, such as the UK Data Protection Act passed in 1984, addressed many of these criticisms. The Act placed a responsibility on all organizations involved in the processing of data relating to identifiable individuals, to meet the requirements of the Act by appointing a data controller and registering their databases with an information commissioner. With the growth in networked computers, the focus of concern broadened to include unauthorized access by hackers. An example of this type of legislation is the Computer Misuse Act, passed in 1990, which makes it an offence in the UK to access another person's computer, or alter data on their computer, without the owner's permission. The growth of the Internet has given rise to the term *cybercrime* – the use of a computer to carry out criminal activity – and increasingly, national laws are being passed to prevent this.

This brings us to another source of computer-related legislation, namely international treaties and conventions. A very good example is an international agreement called the Council of Europe Convention on Cybercrime. This treaty was aimed particularly at countries which have not yet updated their legal framework to reflect the complexities of the Internet. The crimes are divided into a number of different categories: these are data crimes, network crimes, access crimes and other related crimes. *Data crimes* relate to the theft or deliberate modification of data. *Network crimes* involve interfering with a network to prevent access or sabotaging a network. *Access crimes* include gaining unauthorized access to systems and the introduction of viruses, Trojans, worms or other types of malware. The *Other related crimes category* includes forgery, fraud, and other existing crimes which are carried out with the assistance of a computer. This can include phishing attempts, where forged e-mails are sent to trick users into logging on to fake websites which then steal their usernames and passwords.

The Council of Europe Convention on Cybercrime requires countries to respond to requests from other countries to investigate breaches of the law. However, this requirement has caused considerable controversy as there is no requirement that the law in the investigating country has been broken. A spokesperson for the US-based Electronic Frontier Foundation, or EFF, gave the example of the French government requesting the investigation of a US citizen offering Nazi memorabilia for sale over the Internet, which is legal in the US but illegal in France. The EFF spokesperson went on to say, in an article on a news website called ZDNet news, that he has no doubt that a country which signs up to the treaty is being asked, and I quote, "to spy on its citizens."

Another area where international treaty-based law is being created is in relation to copyright or intellectual property, which has been a controversial area for some time. The World Intellectual Property Organization – or WIPO for short – is a UN organization based in Switzerland and is responsible for a number of treaties which address copyright issues. However, some people say that when these treaties have been passed into law by governments, they have ended up protecting only the rights of the copyright holders and ignoring the rights of those who purchase material protected by copyright. Of course, copyright holders must be protected, but their rights need to be balanced against the rights of others. The evidence shows that this is especially true with respect to the US. In my view, the Digital Millennium Copyright Act, or DMCA, which was passed in the US in 1998, is a case in point. By making it a criminal offence to produce or disseminate technology to help users avoid digital rights management protection, it has damaged innovation. It has also acted as a direct challenge to those who believe that there should be no restrictions on the copying of content, as a matter of principle. A very interesting article by Steven

Furnell and others, called "Dissecting the 'Hacker Manifesto'," gives an extremely good insight into what actually motivates these individuals.

In addition, there are those who believe that the legislation unfairly infringes the individual's right to back up material which they have already purchased. This has been the subject of a considerable number of legal challenges. In the EU, the same treaties have been implemented in the European Copyright Directive, or EUCD. This directive also imposes considerable restrictions on the rights of individuals to copy digital content, and is seen by some people as infringing considerably on personal freedoms. Perhaps because of this, there was a considerable delay in implementing the directive into the national law of individual countries.

There are also a number of other points for computer professionals to take into account regarding non-criminal or civil law, which I am only going to touch on here. If you want to look more closely at these, a very good resource is Lloyd's *Information Law* – I'll give you the reference later. A key issue here is *contract law.* Different types of contract which are relevant include an employment contract, which sets out an agreement between a computer professional and the company that employs him or her, or a sales or maintenance contract between two companies for the design, development or maintenance of a computer system. The employment contract determines what is expected of employees, and if they don't meet these expectations, then they will be in breach of contract and can be sacked. Where two companies have a contract for the development of a system, there may be disagreements in terms of whether the quality of the system was in line with expectations. Where such disputes occur, contract law is what determines how the agreement is interpreted. *Civil law* can also be used in other ways. For example, individuals may claim for damages under civil law if they feel that they have been harmed by a product or service. They can also use the civil courts if they feel that their rights have been infringed, for example in the case of a breach of their privacy. An important point to note is that civil law varies considerably between countries, and it's essential that computer professionals are aware of the general provisions of civil law in the countries in which they are working.

Now I'm going to pause at this point and …

Unit 11, Lesson 2, Exercise F 🎧 2.15

However, some people say that when these treaties have been passed into law by governments, they have ended up protecting only the rights of the copyright holders and ignoring the rights of those who purchase copyrighted material. Of course, copyright holders must be protected, but their rights need to be balanced against the rights of others. The evidence shows that this is especially true with respect to the US. In my view, the Digital Millennium Copyright Act, or DMCA, which was passed in the US in 1998, is a case in point. By making it a criminal offence to produce or disseminate technology to help users avoid digital rights management protection, it has damaged innovation. It has also acted as a direct challenge to those who believe that there should be no restrictions on the copying of content, as a matter of principle. A very interesting article by Steven Furnell and others, called "Dissecting the 'Hacker Manifesto'," gives an extremely good insight into what actually motivates these individuals.

Unit 11, Lesson 2, Exercise G 🎧 2.16

Extract 1

Don't misunderstand me, I don't want you to assume that ethics are relevant only when making decisions in the workplace.

Extract 2

As we all know, to some degree, ethical considerations will form a part of every decision you make in your life.

Extract 3

However, it is fair to say that, in the workplace, computer professionals have to be careful that they can't be accused of negligence when designing or operating systems which have an effect on human life or property.

Extract 4

So in an attempt to keep the discussion on professional responsibility reasonably simple, I'm going to …

Extract 5

The greatest fear initially was of a 'Big Brother' society, that is to say a society in which the government would know everything about its citizens and could exercise total control over them.

Extract 6

Public concern regarding government use of information from citizens grew to the extent that the Privacy Act was passed in 1974.

Extract 7

The Act was criticized, however, because it was difficult to enforce and, not only that, but because it excluded the collection of data by companies and organizations other than government.

Extract 8

Daniel Solove gives a good description of the issues around this in his 2004 book on technology and privacy in the information age.

Extract 9

Briefly, in his chapter on information privacy law, he explains how the many exemptions and loopholes in the Act meant that it did not fully address the concerns which had led to it being passed.

Extract 10

The EFF spokesperson went on to say, in an article on a news website called ZDNet news, that he has no doubt that a country which signs up to the treaty is being asked, and I quote, "to spy on its citizens".

Extract 11

The evidence shows that this is especially true with respect to the US.

Extract 12

In my view, the Digital Millennium Copyright Act, or DMCA, which was passed in the US in 1998, is a case in point.

Unit 11, Lesson 3, Exercise A 🎧 2.17

,disciplinary 'action

'black ,hat

i'dentity ,theft

de,nial of 'service

'software ex,ploit

,social engi'neering

i,llegal ac'tivities

'bulletin ,board

Unit 11, Lesson 3, Exercise B 🎧 2.18

Part 3

Let's turn now to the ways in which regulations, as opposed to law, can be used to help in decision-making. As you will be aware, most companies will have a wide range of regulations. These are designed to provide guidance in decision-making in areas where there may be differences of opinion. So, how important is complying with company regulations? First of all, there is no question that this is a good idea if you want to keep your job. We have to accept, as employees, that there are certain things which computer professionals can and cannot do. But the question is, is it enough to follow company rules in order to ensure that decisions are ethical? Some computer professionals claim that they don't have to worry about breaking national and international laws if they follow an employer's instructions. But I'm afraid that just isn't true. It's quite clear that companies can and do do things which are illegal. Research into IT companies and the law has shown that there are instances where companies' actions can be seen as breaking the law. Evidence to support this comes from actual legal cases. A company called Logistep, for example, was found to have infringed privacy laws. Employees posed as users of a peer-to-peer service in order to gather evidence of copyright material being downloaded. A peer-to-peer service – if you're not familiar with this term – is a network of computers for sharing material such as music, film and computer programs, without the need for a central server. When the Logistep employees demanded the users' names and addresses from their ISP, the judge found that the company had breached the privacy to which individuals were entitled. You can see, therefore, why it was important for computer professionals at Logistep to be able to show that their decisions were reasonable, and within the law as they understood it.

A different aspect of this type of situation can be seen in the purchase of a 'botnet' for a BBC programme on computer security in 2009. Botnets, a shortened version of robot networks, are groups of computers on which hackers have managed to install software without their owners' consent. The computers can then be used by the hackers for illegal activities. These uses can include spamming, denial of service attacks or as a base for further attacks on other computers. Apparently, botnets are sometimes made available to other hackers for a fee. In this case, the BBC purchased a botnet and used it to show how it could be used for spamming and denial of services. When they had finished, they left a message on the computers which were part of the botnet, alerting them to the fact that their computers had been hacked. However, as a number of experts pointed out, the BBC had clearly broken the law by doing this. In the words of one security expert, "the Computer Misuse Act, passed in 1990, makes it an offence in the UK to access another person's computer, or alter data on their computer, without the owner's permission." Clearly, computer professionals employed by the BBC in relation to this project could try to avoid disciplinary action by arguing that they were following their employer's instructions. However, as a criminal prosecution was a possibility, they should also be able to show that they had fully considered the implications of their decision. In the event, the BBC was not prosecuted as it was felt that the use of real botnets in the programme had helped more home computer users take their online security more seriously.

So, if employers' rules are not enough, then what other types of rules can be used? Well, almost all the main professional associations have their own ethical guidelines, and these can help in checking decision-making. Some examples of these are the British Computer Society and the Institute of Electrical and Electronics Engineers. Although some people may claim that guidelines are often ignored by their members, they offer a good way for computer professionals to evaluate how ethical their decisions are, regardless of their specific employment context.

A very good example of a situation where decisions have to be constantly evaluated is where computer security companies engage in ethical hacking. This is where security company employees with high-level computer skills are given the job of trying to break into their clients' systems in order to test their security. Sometimes this is done using social engineering, pretending to be somebody in the company in order to get access to usernames and passwords. But sometimes it is technical, where hackers make use of known software exploits – that is, flaws in the software which allow them to take control of a system.

The employees who participate in this sort of penetration testing are often known as 'white hat' hackers, like the good guys in the old cowboy movies. The hackers who try to gain unauthorized access to systems in order to commit crimes are known as 'black hats', the bad guys. Black hats routinely break the law and engage in behaviour which is very questionable, ethically speaking. However, there are times when some of a white hat hacker's behaviour crosses over the line and laws are broken. Hackers who find themselves in this situation are called 'grey hat' hackers, and while they may break the law, research has concluded that they provide a very valuable role. The evidence lies in the fact that 'grey hat' hackers continue to be used by large companies in order to identify the flaws in their own computer security.

Now I'm going to set you a task which will involve investigating some of the points I've raised. I want you to do some research into the issues related to ethical hacking. I want you to focus, firstly, on some of the legal implications of ethical hacking, with respect to the legislation we've discussed. Secondly, I'd like you to think about whether company rules and regulations can cover all of the possibilities when employees are engaged in ethical hacking, and if not, what companies can do to make sure they are covered. Finally, I would like you to look at justifications put forward by hackers for their illegal activity.

Unit 11, Lesson 3, Exercise E 🎧 2.19

But the question is, is it enough to follow company rules in order to ensure that decisions are ethical? Some computer professionals claim that they don't have to worry about breaking national and international laws if they follow an employer's instructions. But I'm afraid that just isn't true. It's quite clear that companies can and do do things which are illegal. Research into IT companies and the law has shown that there are instances where companies' actions can be seen as breaking the law. Evidence to support this comes from actual legal cases. A company called Logistep, for example, was found to have infringed privacy laws. Employees posed as users of a peer-to-peer service in order to gather evidence of copyright material being downloaded. A peer-to-peer service – if you're not familiar with this term – is a network of computers for sharing material such as music, film and computer programs, without the need for a central server. When the Logistep employees demanded the users' names and addresses from their ISP, the judge found that the company had breached the privacy to which individuals were entitled. You can see, therefore, why it was important for computer professionals

at Logistep to be able to show that their decisions were reasonable, and within the law as they understood it.

Unit 11, Lesson 4, Exercise E 🎧 2.20

Extract 1

MAJED: The lecturer we listened to last week introduced a number of interesting issues. In my part of the seminar, I'd like to start by explaining some relevant legal issues regarding ethical or white hat hacking techniques. You might think that because a client has given their consent for the hacking, then it will be considered a legal act. For example, when an ethical hacker hacks a target system in the UK, with client consent, they could not be prosecuted under the Computer Misuse Act because they have the owner's permission. However, there are other ways in which the hacker can break the law. For example, if the hackers install a keylogger on a computer to gain access to passwords and accidentally collect some personal information belonging to a company employee, they may be in breach of data protection or privacy legislation. So to sum up, we can say that it's very important that there are guidelines in place to make sure that there are no legal breaches when carrying out penetration testing.

Extract 2

EVIE: OK, Majed made it clear that having a client's permission isn't enough to ensure that all of an ethical hacker's actions are legal. Basically, what this means is that there will be situations where a white hat hacker may cross the line and temporarily become a grey hat. Ideally, this shouldn't be the case, but there may be situations where it's necessary. If this is the case, then the hacker should be aware of the relevant legislation and the extent to which their actions breach it. So what this means in practice is that a computer security company will not only need to provide their employees with guidance on the legal implications of their actions, they will also need to provide guidance on ethical justifications if employees do break the law. The computer professional's code of conduct can also provide some guidance on what is and is not acceptable.

Extract 3

JACK: OK, to continue then, I'm going to expand the topic by mentioning another aspect. This is the role of hackers who are not directly employed by a company. These hackers sometimes make use of an opportunity to hack an unsecured system in order to bring the lack of security to its owner's attention. Let me give an example. In 2000, some hackers gained access to the systems owned by Apache and replaced the Apache logo with a Microsoft one. This was very embarrassing for Apache, as a very large proportion of the websites on the Internet use their software. However, even though the hackers had broken the law by accessing the Apache computers, Apache were happy that the hackers had made them take their system security more seriously. In fact, they even set up a meeting with some of the hackers, so that they could improve their security further. Clearly, the principles of the hackers, in not wanting to do any damage, were key to the successful outcome in this case. Does anybody have any opinions or anything they would like to add?

Extract 4

Leila: Following on from what Jack has said about grey hats hacking systems to highlight security, we can also look at a related type of situation. Here, I'm going to explain the ethical issues around the discovery of an exploit in a piece of software. Many grey hat hackers reverse engineer software in order to discover exploits. For a lot of software, this is technically illegal. However, they justify breaking the law because they say that when they discover exploits, they make them public. Once they are made public, the manufacturers then have to provide patches for them to make sure the software is safe for people to use. If black hat hackers are the only people to discover exploits by reverse engineering, they will not make them public, but will instead use them to hack into systems. So even though they are technically breaking the law by reverse engineering, grey hat hackers argue that they are doing good.